VOICES
IN
VERSE

An anthology of poetry
by Soroptimists worldwide

Compiled by members of
Soroptimist International of Canterbury

Voices in Verse
first published September 2009
by Soroptimist International (Canterbury)

EDITOR: Jacque Emery
DESIGN: Greg Hamerton

For more information visit the Soroptimist UK website:
soroptimist-gbi.co.uk

Print management and distribution by Eternity Press:
info@eternitypress.com
www.eternitypress.com

World Poetry Anthology

BIC: DCQ

ISBN 978-0-9585118-7-2

Printed and bound in Great Britain by
CPI Antony Rowe, Chippenham, Wiltshire

FOREWORD

Voices in Verse is a sparkling collection of poems from all over the world. The poems, all by members of Soroptimist International, demonstrate the warm-hearted values of that organisation. The voices of the poets are linked by their passion for human connection and the world around them and for the importance of the small detail, the small event, against the panorama of nation and history. In the first part of the book, 'Our World', the poems celebrate places – countries like Tajikistan, where eyes 'sparkle with promise'; cities like Port-Louis, where 'time is ajar' and 'amazing Albany'; the 'cathedral floor' of Lake Roitoti in New Zealand; the riot of flowers in a Caribbean garden. The warmth of the writers in their desire to open out and share their homelands is everywhere in the book: 'Would you like to know about my country?' is the inviting start to a poem set in Turkey but it is a question implicitly repeated throughout, a question which draws the reader into a conversation with a host of warm and engaging personalities.

Landscapes and cityscapes are important for revealing relationships and history as in the poem 'Breaker Bay' where an apple-munching child contemplates the view which, we later learn, will not change even when 'other things have.' It is these small details of place which open out into revelatory moments of humanity. We learn of homesickness for Durban triggered by guavas in St Johns Wood High Street. We witness an unexpected moment of grace in a pod on the London Eye and personal triumph on a Cairngorm Crag. We feel the heat of Andalucian passion.

In the second part of the anthology, the members of Soroptimist International share their concerns and passions: for the fragility of the planet, for their relationships with others, for their work and families and for their organisation,

Soroptimist International, which brings them together. It provides a joyful look at some serious topics, a blend of wisdom and playfulness which never fails to charm and engage. In the end, the power of the anthology is not surprising: the biographies of its women contributors are so rich in experience they read like poems, too.

Jo Shapcott
London
August 2009

---

*Poet **Jo Shapcott** was born in London in 1953.*

She was an undergraduate at Trinity College, Dublin.

She teaches on the MA in Creative Writing at Royal Holloway College, University of London and is also Visiting Professor in Poetry at the University of Newcastle and the University of the Arts, London. She is currently President of The Poetry Society.

CONTENTS

The Caribbean

England

The United States of America

OUR THOUGHTS

The Earth – The Environment – Nature

Friendship – Relationships – Love

Work – Family – Life

OUR SOROPTIMISM

INTRODUCTION

Poetry can provide a key to unlock the language of the heart. It reflects the rhythm of being and transcends all national boundaries. It provides a channel for emotions to reach out and touch the reader or listener with an invisible hand.

Voices in Verse is a book of poetry written by Soroptimists from all over the world – 65 poets from 11 countries. Linked by this common bond of communication, its poets emphasise the importance of literacy and the need to foster its development. Women reflect on the beauty of their countryside, proclaim the power of their heritage and identify the problems on their streets. They describe feelings about diet, falling in love at a mature age, and the importance of teamwork. They share a common bond in being members of Soroptimist International, a womens' organisation committed to 'making a difference' in the lives of others.

The members of one club, Canterbury, in the South East of England, invite you to join them on this poetic journey, as you share the laughter and tears of these international *Voices in Verse*.

Voices in Verse

Words jumble in excited profusion,
Spilling out across the naked page.
Voices jar in strange cacophonies,
Sounds overlapping like a raging sea.
Rhythms, metres, swirling soundscapes,
Waves encircling a shrinking world.
Words and voices, calling…echoing…
Sharing universal dreams.
Painted landscapes; heartsliced memories,
Words erupt in shapes of verse.

Jacque Emery (SI Canterbury, England)

OUR WORLD

SOUTH AFRICA

Hilary Semple became a Soroptimist in 1981, and has served on many Executive Committees on the Management Board of Soroptimist International of South Africa. She has held a portfolio called National Editor (writing articles on major South African projects for The Soroptimist) and has also been Friendship Link Co-ordinator for South Africa. At the end of 1999 Hilary retired from the University of the Witwatersrand, Johannesburg, where she was a Senior Lecturer in English Literature. She is the ongoing editor of a Shakespeare Series, and a founder member of the Shakespeare Society of Southern Africa. At the moment Hilary is involved with the University of the Third Age, where she has been giving a course on Shakespeare's plays since U3A's inception in Johannesburg. Hilary lives in a flat in a leafy suburb called Riviera (Johannesburg lies in the largest man-made forest in the world). She is single, goes to art classes, and enjoys being with her friends. She has one brother, who lives in England.

The African Market

As polyphonic as her voices
so the perfumes of Africa:
deep-toned scents, fragrance
black and rich as liquorice,
dark smoky breath of clay pots,
smell of sunrise and sweetgrass,
the aromatic undersong
to the rhythmic beat of *Salsa;*
a suffusion in my blood
inseparable from being.

Hilary Semple (SI Johannesburg, South Africa)

Maimoona's Garden

A salmon-pink wall encloses
a small summer garden,
a rich Tabriz carpet of
trees and flowers springing up
from Earth's matting to the sky;

a birch tree as delicate and slender
as the silken tree from the East
displays its grey-white bark,
and the intricacies of twig and leaf
in tender silver-green on green;

daisies blazon their yellow
symmetry among white roses,
heavy-headed, tangled and twining
in the ancient pattern
of regular irregularity;

the scent of masala tea drifts down
from the stoep together with the
high fluting sound of music,
played by Radio Lotus,
to commingle with the afternoon.

Hilary Semple (SI Johannesburg, South Africa)

There and Here

There
the day hunches against
public monuments,
shifts uncomfortably
against hard edges,
a vagrant
with rheumy eyes.

Clouds move
their grey matter
and ruminate on
the laws of gravity,
sinking lower.

Here
horizons are lines
meeting in infinity,
the endless blue
geometry
of wide angles.

The sky's circumference is
an amplitude of space
and light years,
a brilliant spectrum
of colours
spilling
onto earth.

Hilary Semple (SI Johannesburg, South Africa)

Hannah Lurie *studied part-time at Natal Technical College from 1956-1961 under the tutelage of the sculptress, Mary Stainbank. She is a resident of Durban, South Africa and is a poet and a well known sculptor. She has held numerous solo exhibitions in Durban, Cape Town, Johannesburg and Pretoria, and her work can be seen in many corporate and public galleries throughout South Africa. Her last piece was of two 9-foot-tall bronze figures. Hannah is also a cancer survivor and she has written a little book entitled 'I'm too sexy for my hair', of which 26,000 copies have been circulated free of charge. Inducted as a Soroptimist in 1972, she is a Past President of the Durban Club as well as Past President of Soroptimist International of South Africa. Hannah has three sons, one in Johannesburg, one in London and one in Surrey, England.*

Obituary

Tucked away, page four
bottom right
squeezed
in between Nu Metro cinemas
and below an ad for sweet and sour prawns
the death of Evelyn Rakeepile.

She asked her daughter
on the day she died
to read Psalm 71 verse 9
"Do not throw me away
 in the time of old age;
 just when my power is failing
do not leave me."

Were it Winnie or Brenda Fassie
it would make front page

a visit from a president or two
but the religious first wife
who bore him three children
barely made a news item
three days after her death.

Who is Elizabeth Rakeepile?
Makaziwe informed the newspapers
"My mother died from chronic lung disease."
Makaziwe, the daughter of Madiba,
Rakeepile – the first wife of
Nelson Mandela –
May her soul rest in peace.

Post script: A week later
they attended her funeral
Winnie, Graca and Madiba.
It was a large funeral
I heard about it on the radio
it didn't make *my* daily newspaper
maybe it made yours.

Hannah Lurie (SI Durban, South Africa)

ZIMBABWE

Mary Ndlovu *is Canadian. In 1966, after doing a Master's at Columbia University in New York, she went to teach History, Geography and Civics in a secondary school in Zambia, later becoming a lecturer in the Education Faculty at the University of Zambia. She met her husband, who was a Zimbabwean in exile. They returned to Zimbabwe in 1980 at Independence. He became an opposition MP and was consequently detained in the '80s. He was part of a unity government formed in 1988, but sadly, died the next year. Mary has three children, and four grandchildren, two in Canada and two in South Africa. Mary still lives in Zimbabwe, in Bulawayo, where she taught in a Teachers' College and then worked in a legal services National Government Office, developing a training program for paralegals. She supposedly retired in 2003 but still works as a consultant, because of the lack of pensions. Mary started a library in memory of her husband in the town of Gwanda in Matabeleland South and now has an outreach in many rural villages. She considers herself to be a human rights and social justice activist and she does a lot of voluntary work with a women's organization called WOZA (Women of Zimbabwe Arise) which engages in civil disobedience, promoting freedom of expression and demanding accountability from government. She has been asked to join an Education Advisory Board to advise the new Minister on how to resuscitate the collapsed education system. For the past three years Mary has been President of Soroptimist International, Bulawayo.*

Death Rains

Fields green,
maize stalks swaying,
spiking upwards.
swelling cobs promise
satisfaction, lives well lived.

Cool rain soaks down
runs in streams,
awakening rivers.
Laughter rings as
children's play shapes
dams and roads.

We never listen to the thunder;
lightning's strike is far away –
a distant victim.

Wind's moan begins,
its rising voice,
ascending shrieks
pierce darkened sky.
Towering nimbus
open on us –
spill blood-rain.

No god's hand this
but human devilry
shredding stalks,
crushing cobs
child cut from mother, father felled,
goats and chickens drowned in torrents

Emptying stomachs,
crumbling huts, poisoning wells
flattening hope.

Stealing the promise, the present, the future…

I never told you how I felt
because I couldn't.
No words,
no tears

Mary Ndlovu (SI Bulawayo, Zimbabwe)

MAURITIUS

Jacqueline Pilot *was born in Mauritius where her ancestors settled around 1770. She worked as a teacher, with part-time jobs as a translator and journalist for the first magazine written and edited by women, 'Le Magazine de la Mauricienne'. She has retired now and travels to France and Australia to visit her sisters, as well as taking care of the family home in Mauritius. Jacqueline has written poetry since she was young, inspired and stimulated at home by her mother's mad and passionate love for the Symbolist poets. She has won several awards in Mauritius, and has had poems published regularly in the 'page littéraire' of a local newspaper. The main themes of her work are insular, or express the contrast between city life abroad and life in Mauritius near the sea: her first poetry booklet is titled 'Nord-Sud'. She is a member of SI Ipsae, and she has held several offices, including that of President. She finds poetry fascinating and believes that music and books are almost as important as friends!*

Port-Louis   *Our Capital City*

On the Parade-Ground, against the blue sky,
rows of palms grow tall and fair
like the souls of the Just, luminous and calm
between the rows of palms, stately statues watch.

The gain is heavy on the trestle-tables
Time is ajar, straddled with silence
when the merchants' chests and boxes sleep,
deep in the shady hours.

But light, obliquely striking, stirs up the fire.
And the forefinger of the big banker starts the business again
– gold and silver light up in the hands of the exchangers

and the potter returns to his clay
the merchant to his silk
here's the gossip-writer prowling about his ground
the auction and the town-crier
the minstrel and the fiddler.

Twilight: nimble fingers leaf through
the returns of the day!

Sunset brings back home
the dressy and the dowdy, the bully and the sweetie
the docker and the rambler, the juggler and the canvasser.
Between two cargoes, the seller of fries
offers fat fritters to the hawker.
The water, stale and sour,
mulls its dirty smells over and over.
The betel seller squeezes crumpled papers
with red fingers.
In the slums excitement rises.
In the wings of the square, gamblers lay their stakes.
At the foremast, here's the signal of the supplier.

Tramp tramp tramp
on the parvis of the church
by the ups and downs of his conscience
as he comes and goes
to and fro
the drug-pedlar chooses his side

    Dusty lamps, odd gatherings
    slanting eyes and dull hands on the dice
    one plays Pope Joan before being the King
    before being the knave.
    The soul is so flexible in the streets of the town.

And the island gives birth on every branch
in every nest of love in every nest of hate

it answers pat, it concocts its genes
it cooks its heritage in the sun of marriage
in the fire of heretics
in each Abel a Cain is dozing.

The soul is so flexible in the streets of the town.

✳ ✳ ✳ ✳ ✳

I sow my poem, the minstrel says,
Pick it in the wind
The liar curses it
Remorse comes close behind

The ace of spades tries a new suit for the queen of hearts
the financier makes up his face to beguile the money-lender
the joker clears out to ruin the gambler
the heart flings open for the wangler

And the croupière, stuck to the game, absent-minded
stares at the horizon of her dull and long day
she steers her wheel, her course, her tacks
in the reds and the blacks, watching her rings and her bearings

The tout and the small fry go fidgeting along
weaving a whole network of fear and illusion
they strut and fret and hope they'll soon stir up a throng
each one needs the other – they thrive on collusion

I sow my poem, the minstrel says,
Pick it in the wind
The liar curses it
Remorse comes close behind

The tub-thumper launches his speech
in the rabble's face as in a broth
it cooks and fries in the cheating eyes

in the ravenous hearts of the fishy lot

That bird of ill omen holding out the olive-branch
fidgeting and putting on a show as he whets his sword
gobbling and abusing and double-speaking
it's the big bully, the rattler lining up trophies

When the right hand doesn't know what the left hand does,
it's Pacifex the Liar at the top of his voice
calling out to the crowd, that artless simpleton.
Welcome, all, to the ambidextrous show!

I sow my poem, the minstrel says,
Pick it in the wind
The liar curses it
Remorse comes close behind

        ✶ ✶ ✶ ✶ ✶

Dove, beware the snake, it will eat you!

Here's the Hacker, the double-dealer
His daily bread: the sorrowful and the sickly
the lame in the heart
His choice morsel, his treat: the innocent,
the happy one, the merry-maker

You whistle, you bewitch, you hook and harry,
You worry, you shrink and patch up,
Sometimes you slowly, lengthily spread out your coils
You go on unwinding your sugary speech
While you're tightening your bitter iron-collar.

Snake, beware, the minstrel says,
You'll split and sputter!

On the Parade – Ground against the blue sky,

Rows of palms grow tall and fair
Like the souls of the Just, luminous and calm
Among the rows of palms, stately statues watch …

Jacqueline Pilot (SI Ipsae, Mauritius)

Colombe, Gare Au Serpent
Sur Le Port

Sur la Place d'Armes, contre le bleu du ciel
se dressent des rangées de palmes, hautes et calmes
comme les âmes des Justes, lumineuses et belles
Entre les rangées de palmes, d'augustes statues veillent.

Le gain est lourd sur les tréteaux d'après-midi
à l'heure entrebâillée chevauchée de silence
où dorment scellés d'ombre les coffres des marchands.

Mais la lumière, en ses frontières obliques, en
ranime le feu. Et le doigt sec du grand banquier
relance le trafic
- l'or et l'argent s'allument aux mains des échangeurs.
Et le potier renoue avec la glaise
et le marchand avec la soie
on entend l'échotier qui rôde sur son aire,
on entend la criée avec les accrocheurs
et puis au loin, l'accordeur et le ménétrier.

C'est crépuscule et la rentrée du jour s'effeuille
entre les doigts agiles!
Le coucher du soleil ramène à domicile
et l'élégante et la malmise, et le rustaud et la soumise.
Le débardeur avec le promeneur, le bateleur avec
le démarcheur.
Le friturier au camelot du port offre entre deux cargos
des pâtes blondes et grasses

L'eau galvaudée ressasse ses relents d'outre gavée d'odeurs
Le vendeur de bétel referme ses doigts rouges
sur un papier froissé. On s'émeut
dans les bouges. A l'heure mitoyenne
dans les coulisses de la place les mises
se précisent, Mironton mirontaine,
au grand mât de misaine, c'est le signal du pourvoyeur.
Devant l'église, par les cent pas de sa conscience,
le trafiquant choisit son camp.

    Ampoule poussiéreuse, assemblée rapiécée
    l'oil-miroir et la main fade sur les dés,
    on se fait nain jaune avant d'être le roi
    avant d'être valet
    on a l'âme ductile dans les rues de la ville.

Et l'île enfante à chaque branche
à chaque nid d'amour à chaque nid de haine,
donne la réplique
elle concocte ses gènes
elle cuit ses héritages au soleil du mariage
au feu des hérétiques.
En chaque Abel un Caïn qui sommeille.

    On a l'âme ductile dans les rues de la ville.

       *****

Je sème mon poème dit le ménétrier
Qu'on le cueille en plein vent
Le menteur le fait anathème
Le remords est par-devant

L'as de pique se rhabille pour la dame de cour
l'argentier se maquille pour séduire le prêteur
le joker se défile pour couler le joueur
et le cour s'écarquille pour le resquilleur

Et la croupière rivée au jeu regarde ailleurs
elle dévisage d'un fixe l'horizon de sa journée
elle navigue sa roue, son cap et ses bordées
en pays rouge et noir, de bille en billevesées

Le rabatteur et le fretin
vont de conserve en frétillant
ils vont tissant de leurs secrets
tout un réseau de boniments

Je sème mon poème dit le ménétrier
Qu'on le cueille en plein vent
Le menteur le fait anathème
Le remords est par-devant

Le harangueur lance sa verve
dans un bouillon de populace
elle saisit elle fricasse
dans l'oil véreux dans l'oil vorace

Cet oiseau de malheur qui brandit l'olivier
qui s'agite à l'envi aiguisant son épée
qui glousse et qui houspille d'une voix biseautée
c'est le grand ferrailleur alignant les trophées

Lorsque la dextre ignore ce que fait la senestre
c'est Pacifex le Faux rameutant à tue-tête
la foule bisonne la pauvre biscornue.
à la farce ambidextre soyez les bienvenus!

Je sème mon poème dit le ménétrier
Qu'on le cueille en plein vent
Le menteur le fait anathème
Le remords est par-devant

*****

Colombe, gare au serpent, il te mangera!

Voici le pourfendeur à la langue fourchue
Son ordinaire, son quotidien: le débile, le chagrin,
celui qui boîte du cour.
Son mets de choix: l'innocent, le joyeux,
l'artisan du bonheur.

Tu siffles, tu fascines, tu harponnes, tu taquines,
tu chiffonnes, tu rapetisses et rapetasses,
parfois tu étends lentement longuement tes
anneaux,
tu t'en vas déroulant ton argument de miel,
tu t'en vas resserrant ton carcan de fiel.

Serpent, gare à toi, dit le ménétrier,
Tu dégorgeras!

Sur la Place d'Armes, contre le bleu du ciel
se dressent des rangées de palmes, hautes et calmes
comme les âmes des Justes, lumineuses et belles
Entre les rangées de palmes, d'augustes statues veillent …

Jacqueline Pilot (SI Ipsae, Mauritius)

TAJIKISTAN

Lois A. Herman *is Coordinator of the Women's UN Report Network (WUNRN), which is one of the largest and most active global gender resource programs. WUNRN addresses the rights, oppression, and empowerment of women and girls all over the world and operates a daily information service that goes throughout the UN system and enters over three–quarters of UN countries. Lois is a Gender Specialist. In the past two years, she has founded the WUNRN European Office in Italy. She speaks regularly at the United Nations and Conferences, and has received several Awards. Lois is a member of Soroptimist International of Greater Minneapolis, USA. She has also visited Soroptimist clubs in at least 9 countries. Lois is a widow and has four children. Her poem, Tajik Girl, was written and read by Lois at the closing of the WUNRN-MODAR Conference on Gender Inequalities in Education (in Dushanbe, Tajikistan, 2006).*

Tajik Girl

Tajik girl, your eyes sparkle with promise.
Your mind is clear and inquisitive.
You want to learn!

Tajik girl, education is your human right.
You are a spirit of hope and opportunity
For your family, your community, your country.

Tajik girl, follow your dreams.
Stay in school; study well; keep good values.
You are special and important for the future of Tajikistan!

Lois Herman (SI Greater Minneapolis, Minnisota, USA)

AUSTRALIA

Bronwyn O'Shannessy *was born in 1949 and her home town is Quairading which is 160 kms east of Perth, Western Australia. It is a mixed farming area and her brothers still maintain the family farming tradition. Bronwyn is married and has been been residing in Albany since July 2002, having moved from Northam, where she had worked in Local Government as Secretary to the CEO. Now she is enjoying an excellent climate along with some beautiful coastal scenery. Bronwyn works full time as a legal secretary. She has been a member of SI Albany for 3 years and Club Secretary for two of them. She loves gardening. She has a cat named Alby (because she was abandoned in Albany) who rules the house!*

Albany

A is for Amazing Albany on the south coast of Western Australia

L is for the love we have for Soroptimists and our sisters all over the world

B is for being there for family, friends and the community

A is for awareness of what makes a difference

N is for new horizons as we reach out with Programme Action.

Y is for You as we welcome everyone to our special part of this beautiful country.

Bronwyn O'Shannessy (SI Albany, Western Australia)

NEW ZEALAND

Joan Lees *is an ex-teacher who has written since childhood. She is a charter member of Soroptimist International of Waimea (in Richmond, Nelson, New Zealand). It was formed in 1974 and belongs to the Region of New Zealand South, and the Federation of the South-West Pacific. Joan has been Club President, and she has attended various conferences as a club delegate. Her other interests are Girl Guiding, church, family and Scottish country dancing. Joan's poem 'Weaving' is about the various races who have made New Zealand their home over the past 20 years. 'Lakeside Shrine' and 'Flight' are both set in the Nelson Lakes National Park, which is about one and a half hours' drive from her home in Stoke, Nelson.*

Lakeside Shrine – Lake Rotoiti

Stretched at the mountain's base
lies a lake of pewter,
a cathedral floor, calm and marble grey.
Shorewards, ashine through shallows,
a muted mosaic of stones rims
the wooded aisle we tread.
Earth's incense drifts
through sun-dappled space
to the leaf-studded roof,
stayed by live tree pillars.
Somewhere in the choir stalls
birdsong falls in golden notes.
The carpet of last year's spring
hushes the footsteps, stifles
the voices to reverence.

Joan Lees (SI Waimea, New Zealand)

Weaving

Weave me a korowai,
   cloak of nobility;
tangata whenua
   came here of old.
Weave me kimonos,
   silk of the Orient,
Saris and sarongs
   brilliant with gold.
Weave tweed from Donegal.
   Bannockburn, Harris,
sturdy, hard-wearing,
   keeping out cold.
Weave lacy filigree,
   Honiton, Mechlin,
finer than cobwebs,
   dainty to hold.
Weave into unity
   strands of humanity;
weave peace and harmony
   all men to enfold.

Joan Lees (SI Waimea, New Zealand)

Flight

Helicopter shudders, lifts off.
We watch its dragonfly shadow
drift like thistledown far below.

Circle the lake, sun splinters
on wooded shoreline and mountains.
Wing towards the lake's head, weave through
rocky defiles to reach hidden
country beyond, wild and remote.
Snow on alpine plateaux lies deep;
beneath, in forested gorges,
silver rivers thread the shadows,
slide towards the lake, where huts cling
to ferny bank and narrow beach:
safe havens for weary trampers.
Mountain peaks rear snowy summits
into the void. Cloud wisps obscure
their dizzy heights, their craggy steeps,
make of this land a mystery,
an unknown, untried wilderness.

Helicopter sinks down, settles
on familiar earth again.
The world's routines envelop us.

Joan Lees (SI Waimea, New Zealand)

Frances Meech *was born in New Zealand in 1946. She is*
university educated and a trained teacher with a Certificate in
Community Services. Frances belongs to the New Zealand Poetry
Society and she has published five collections of poetry. She is
involved in her local Catholic parish, and joined Soroptimist
International in 1996, initially at Wellington East, now at
Wellington. She has been married to Peter for forty-two years
and they have three children and seven grandchildren. Frances
enjoys walking her dog and loves the peace and quiet of their
Marlborough Sounds retreat.

Breaker Bay

Breaker Bay tucked away
at the entrance to Wellington harbour

here before tangata whenua
likely to remain

long after current generations have gone
unless an earthquake of 1855 dimensions

remodels our coastline
as a child I walked with my father

taking an apple to munch
contemplating the view

southwards the rocks of Barrett's Reef
often appear innocuous

but in a southerly gale
they tore the bottom out of the Wahine

in what we now call last century – 1968
after a southerly surfers ride the break

on calm days the blue and white flag
warns of divers beneath

the view has not changed
but other things have

Dad long gone, myself half a century older
hopefully wiser

I still enjoy walking your shore
rambling with my dog

never quite sure what we might find
occasionally a seal, a dead bird

or remains of a fish
in summer a nude sunbather

somehow similar to the seal
reinforcing Darwin's theories

I hope to continue my walks
for the remainder of my days

Breaker Bay I expect
to stay much the same

Frances Meech (SI Wellington, New Zealand)

Queen Charlotte Sound

Down the Sounds at Maraetai Bay
the evening breeze
the water lapping in towards us
with the chill of iced cucumber
on the flesh
the boat in, the fishing done
at dark a gas light held high
illuminated your surgeon's hands
filleting Blue Cod, Tarakihi, Moki, Gurnard
on the rocky foreshore beside the jetty
like a primitive fisherman
bringing home food and more
We all stood in the coolness
of the night
with the swarming sandflies
fogging around us
until the fish were piled on plates
a brief walk through the bush
to the bach
to feast on kaimoana

Frances Meech (SI Wellington, New Zealand)

The New Zealand Bach

Old furniture, old clothes
older ourselves

comfortable
more comfortable

than our city home
is our recycled home, the bach

Frances Meech (SI Wellington, New Zealand)

THE CARIBBEAN: BARBADOS

Pansy Lineth Griffith *(née Adams) lives in the West Indies. She was born in 1943 on the island of Grenada but now lives in Barbados. She is a parent and has two sons. Pansy has now retired after 35 years, but worked as a specialist in early childhood education. She taught Reception and Kindergarten classes at St. Gabriel's Primary School and launched and operated 'Aunty Pansy's Day Care Centre'. As her poem 'My Garden' reflects, Pansy loves flowers and is a member of Barbados Flower Arranging Society, and was the President in 2000-2003. She is also a member of Barbados Horticultural Society, Barbados Association of Flower Arrangers, Grenada Association of Flower Arrangers and The World Association of Flower Arrangers. She is also a Cub Scouts Leader and a Family and Social Counsellor. Pansy is a committed Soroptimist and is in her second term as President of SI Barbados – hosting the SIGBI conference in 2008. Pansy's hobbies include cooking, swimming, walking, singing, gardening, reading and traveling. She is a crossword puzzle enthusiast, and loves opera and theatre.*

My Garden

Beauty, beauty everywhere
Flowers blooming oh, so fair
Would you like to have a peek
Of what is blossoming this week?

Look at this Heliconia – yellow and erect
And cousin Rostrata, his thin neck flexed
Supporting the fuzzy red petals edged with yellow –
Indeed, a very unique fellow

Ginger Lilies – reds, pinks, and whites
And heart-shaped Anthuriums dancing in the light
A bunch of Ixora making enough room
To shelter the Tuberose with her delicate perfume.

Look, the magnificent Orchids – the heart-throb of most
How beautiful and varied – mind if I boast?
Desert Roses, Hibiscus, Crotons, Irises
And the various Greens of the Foliages.

My Garden keeps me wonderfully happy
Especially being a member of our Flower Arranging Society
From Barbados to Chelsea – Gold Awards are won
When gardens like mine blossom in the Barbadian sun.

Pansy Griffith (SI Barbados)

ENGLAND

Su Rennison *was born in Halifax, Yorkshire, England. She was brought up in Worcestershire but has lived in Kent for most of her working life. Su has had two careers. The first as Tutor-Librarian working in Higher Education Colleges. The second as the Christian Stewardship Adviser for the Church of England Diocese of Canterbury. A Soroptimist since her early thirties, Su has been President of SI Canterbury twice (1979-80 and 1987-88). Su is married to John. They both enjoy reading, walking and the theatre. As amateur musicians playing 'cello and viola they have been described as 'the back legs of a String Quartet!'*

The London Eye

Man-made for the millennium
The majestic eye moves through time
Unceasing in its own silence
Seeing with many human eyes
The grace and beauty of the man made city
Shimmering in the sheen of a winter sun.

Lethargic and lazy the River Thames
Like a coiled serpent sits in the sun.
Unruffled by the chugging boats,
Or the bridges anchored to its sides –
Lambeth, Westminster and Waterloo
Evoking Britain's past anew.

On the Embankment walk Lowry men
Lowry size and shape in living form
Not caught on canvas ere the Eye was born,
But bewitched here, now, for eyes
Aware, they too will look as such to others
Once released again to join their brothers.

Charing Cross Station is hurling out
Hornby trains set on children's rails
To rattle unheard across The Thames
To myriad stations and destinations,
Unnamed, unknown, left to wander
By wondering eyes greedy for London.

In the heart of the City lies St. Paul's
A brave beacon from a bygone age.
Protected by skyscrapers tall and proud
Symmetrical boxes, circles, and squares,
Blanched white concrete in a glistening light
Radiant by day sparkling by night.

Yet what of me cocooned in a capsule
Spellbound with wonder, joy and awe
Suspended in space and out of time
Filled with exquisite exhilaration –
At so much beauty, so much brightness
Overflowing bounty laid at my feet?

A surge of thanksgiving fills my soul,
For the gracious gift of man to man
Yet offered to God as Man's creator,
Who surely revels in His children's skill
With metal, concrete, glass and stone
And will take and bless it as His own.

Su Rennison (SI Canterbury, England)

St. John's Wood

I walk down St. John's Wood High Street –
I'm happy – hugely happy,
even the sun is out today.
I shut my eyes and savour the warmth
of late Spring.
Abbey Road, where the Beatles record their music
is on the next street,
I softly sing
"She loves me yeah, yeah, yeah"
and walk into Tesco's on the corner
to shop for my weekend groceries.
And then a familiar tin
imprints on my memory.
I've lived happily in London
for three years
yet this tin – Silver Leaf –
has caught my attention like no other.
I pick it up and read –
'Koejawels' – guavas –
My whole being goes into spasm!
I throw it down and run out of the shop.
On St. John's Wood pavement
I stand and weep –
"My dear, can I help?"
a kind woman offers
"No," I sob, "No thank you,
I'm just being really silly."
I would never have thought
I was homesick
but 'Koejawels' did it for me.
I dry my tears,
walk back
and try to ignore
the Silver Leaf shelf.

Hannah Lurie (SI Durban, South Africa)

Betty Martin *is a 'Gravesend shrimp'. She was born in Gravesend, Kent, England in 1928 and she still lives there. She was evacuated on the day that World War 2 began and travelled on the Royal Sovereign Paddle Steamer down the River Thames, into the North Sea and up the coast to Great Yarmouth. She spent six months in West Runton and seven months in Diss, East Anglia, before returning home to Gravesend. Betty trained to be a teacher at Stockwell College in Bromley, Kent and then went back to Gravesend! Betty is a Lay Reader in the Church of England and became a Soroptimist in 1977 under that category. She was President of her club between 1991-1992. Betty has made Soroptimist friends in many parts of Europe, including Denmark, Germany and Switzerland. She still loves being a Soroptimist because of its ideals and the love and fun that is shared between members.*

Memories: Opposite 63 Bayswater Road

Chestnut candles pointing to the sky
Unseen by people hurrying by.
Motor cycle outriders in fluorescent green
Off to the palace to see the Queen.
Kensington Gardens off Bayswater Road
Many years ago my children I showed.

I cross the road and enter the park
Watching the people and dogs that bark.
Horses canter with tails streaming;
Riders' black boots all shining and gleaming
Remind me that once I used to ride
Will I do it again, no fear, I decide.

There's Peter Pan's statue all shiny and brown
Smiling at children as they run around.
My own two children have polished those toes
Have their children seen him – I don't think so.

There's the round pond where we sailed the boats
That got stuck in the weeds – took ages to refloat.
Those boats are in the cupboard up in the loft
With puppets, pogo stick and toys all soft.
Together with photos and rubber mini brix
That Angela used to smell – they gave her a fix.

My memories are jingling like bells that ring
As squirrels scamper and the birds still sing
But it's time to leave. From the park I go
I long to linger but it can't be so.

Soroptimist meeting in a hot sticky room
But thanks for the memories 'chestnuts in bloom'.

Betty Martin (SI Gravesend and District, England)

Jacque Emery *was born in 1949 in Herne Bay, Kent, England.
She trained as a professional singer at The Royal Academy
of Music in London and also has Diplomas in Drama from
LAMDA and a Masters' Degree in Theology and Education from
Liverpool University. Jacque has worked as a teacher in a variety
of schools and became Deputy Headteacher of a Comprehensive
school in Hertfordshire. In 1988 she became an Education
Adviser for Drama, Music and Religious Education in Sefton.
She has been an external examiner for LAMDA since 1978 and
also an Ofsted School Inspector. Jacque is currently Syllabus
Manager and Chief Examiner for LAMDA Examinations. She
has written two books of poetry for children, various educational
articles, playscripts and songs. She recently contributed to
a book on the history of Musical Theatre. Attracted by the
international dimension of Soroptimism, she joined SI Bootle
and was President from 2003-2004. She is now a member of SI
Canterbury. Jacque loves to travel and has a house in Benahavis,
Spain. She likes photography and reading – when she has time!
Jacque is single and lives with two pampered Persian cats.*

The Pilgrims' Way

Cries of horses, traders, merchants,
Jostling crowds in livery splendours,
Well-wimpled ladies, knights in armour,
Worthy countries' gallant defenders.
Doctors, plowmen, clerks and nobles,
Pilgrim footprints, in rain-spattered line,
Begging friars and cowled religious
Patchwork of people to Canterbury's shrine.

Single track on time-washed pathway,
Booming birds in grass-hidden lairs,
Nothing but shadows and nothing but whispers,
Echoes of penitents whispering prayers.
Ghostly cries of supplication,
Cries from both joyful and broken hearted.
Where are the pilgrims to this ancient city?
Dead they may be: they have not departed.

Jacque Emery (SI Canterbury, England)

Marie Blacktop *was born in Blackburn, England and has lived in the Ribble Valley in Lancashire for 38 years. She was a teacher for 33 years, and latterly, Deputy Head of a comprehensive school until she took early retirement. Since then she has been a volunteer at a local primary school helping with their reading partnership scheme. Marie is married to Roy and they celebrate their Ruby Wedding in July 2009. They have two children and two grandchildren. Marie joined Blackburn Soroptimists 12 years ago and has been Club President, Regional Press and Publicity Officer, Regional Vice-President, Regional President Elect and is currently Regional President for North West England and the Isle of Man. Marie enjoys walking, theatre, reading, and travel and is a life-long supporter of Blackburn Rovers football club.*

Memories of Blackburn past

The butcher's stall my grandfather ran,
Selling choice cuts of meat on market day.
I loved to watch him sharpen the blade,
Knife poised each time a new customer came
Asking for neck, shank, leg, brisket or silverside.

The stall pitched on the same spot each week,
The end of a row in prime position
As befits the town's longest-standing tenant,
But cold and wet in winter months
When hands were warmed on jugs of tea
And feet stamped to keep the blood circulating.

When Easter came everything changed:
The stall was moved to another site
Making way for the annual Fair
Whose sounds and smells I can still recall,
The banging and knocking, each ride put in place,

Experts shouting directions to local amateur helpers,
Generators throbbing and whirring
Bringing life to rides and sideshows
The aroma of candy floss, toffee apples and frying onions.

The excitement when all was ready
Sweethearts holding hands and stealing kisses
Under the cover of the caterpillar hood,
Girls squealing louder and louder on the waltzer
Making the youth whip the rides round faster and faster
Showing off as he stepped from one to the next
Nonchalantly combing his sleeked-back hair.

Something for the parents too,
The pot fair, where gravel-voiced men
Threw baskets of cups and plates one to the other,
Offering free cream jug and basin to the first to buy,
Producing oohs and aahs from wide-eyed onlookers
Waiting for breakages and spills that never came.

Soon all was over and normal life resumed.
The fairground people left – off to the next town,
Leaving behind a few broken hearts, some dreams
Of those who envied their nomadic life,
And stall holders relieved to take back their own pitch again,
My grandfather foremost among them.

Marie Blacktop (SI Blackburn, England)

Brenda Lynton Escreet *was born in 1947 in Morecambe,*
Lancashire, England. She was adopted and grew up in Kirkby
Lonsdale and Lancaster. She is married to Malcolm, an Engineer
and they have four children, four granddaughters, three
grandsons, three handsome cats and a feisty Italian greyhound!
Brenda worked for Lancashire Youth & Community Service for
twenty eight years, and has been a member of SI Morecambe
& Heysham for eleven years. She was club President in 2002.
In 1996,following two working visits to Swaziland with 'Sharing
the Challenge', a young peoples HIV/AIDS prevention project,
Brenda founded PIES, (Partners in Education Swaziland)and
she is currently Chair of Trustees. A passionate Disability
activist, she has Multiple Sclerosis, Brenda is very committed
to the promotion of equality for women and girls. She has
written poetry for at least forty years, and would recommend
it to all Soroptimists, encouraging them to 'just pick up a pen!'
The following poem was written on a journey from her office in
Preston to Colne, a small town on the edge of the Pennines just
before Christmas. There had been a heavy fall of snow.

New Age Traveller

Unfocused, I gaze through the window as the shabby carriages
    lurch over the rural track.
Familiar sights float in and out of view, rendered unfamiliar by
    an early, unseasonal, fall of snow.
The cows that fill these fields, lifting incurious heads in the
    soupy summer air, are hidden away in their steamy, fragrant
    warmth, until a far-away spring liberates them.

Across the golf links…an essential crop for farmers who must
    diversify or die…slots left by sporting hares bisect the
    eighteenth hole and leave the bare hillocks to hungry rabbits
    and a single truant cat.
Further on, the train passes a rundown garage.
A woman pauses by an open blue door laden down with snow
    touched greenery.
The shadows swallow her and her garlands as the train rounds
    the bend.

Hurrying by, a few miles to the East, travellers use the new
    motorway.
Swift, efficient, anonymous, bypassing this corner of ancient
    countryside
anxious always to be somewhere else, leaving behind them
    exhaust fumes and the stress of necessary travel.
Nearing my journey's end I snuggle down into the plush,
    scratchy seat.
Certain for these last few minutes that I am still part of a more
    natural world resonant with a purpose that knows how to
    respond to these ancient cycles.

Brenda Lynton-Escreet (SI Morecambe & Heysham, England)

Clare Harding *was born in Louth, Lincolnshire, England, but now lives in Blackburn, Lancashire. She worked as a teacher for 12 years and then spent 21 years working as a teacher / tutor for the National Childbirth Trust. She is now 'retired' and has a new career as a Desktop Publisher! She has one son, an ecologist, now training to be a teacher. Clare only joined SI Blackburn just over a year ago. She is their Press & Publicity Officer, and gets very excited about the regional competitions! Clare loves classical especially religious music, walking, natural history, and writing. Her poetry reflects a very personal picture of landscape. Most relate to places she has known and loved, particularly as a naturalist and walker. '50:50/5' and 'From one who swears not by the Moon' provide an even more personal reaction to an internal landscape: reaction to the diagnosis of cancer and a description of what it felt like to be undergoing chemotherapy. The poem 'Cairngorm' presents Clare's exultation at managing to climb again, during treatment, a favourite mountain, Cairngorm.*

Bon vacance!

Winter and spring wage war
over the wrinkled reddened skin
of ancient sandstone;
flinging a fusillade of hail
on the frost-scorched heather,
wind cleaves to the bone,
covert streams mutter mutinies,
the invading infantry of bracken
infiltrated by wild hyacinth, heads bowed.

White puffs of bog-cotton drift
from the bristling artillery of skirmishing *Scirpus*,
spurred on by butterwort
Polytrichum marches in saffron helmets of calyptra.

Snipe sentries call chikka-challenges
dive-bomb the bogs,
drumming up the advance with strafing tail coverts,
a mournful golden plover bugles the retreat,
pipits parachute behind enemy lines.
The trespass detonates an avian land-mine,
brushing the boots, but still
it takes moments to spot the nest,
tussock-tucked, four camouflaged eggs
cup-cradled in woven fescue.

The black velvet of *Dicranum*
moss-margining a stone recalls
your delicacy of touch, dark gaze.
It is Sunday –
The weather has worn a boulder
to a stone man, bent in prayer.
Briefly I join him,
send you the Peace.

Clare Harding (SI Blackburn, England)

Eskeleth
Arkengarthdale

Autumn has torched the dale,
while above the moors rust into winter.
A berserker's wind rips stark reality from dreams,
rending the misty tissue of lost hope.
Corpse candles light the plaited, pyre-bound warrior
on his final voyage.

Clare Harding (SI Blackburn, England).

Notes on a Cornish Spring
Loe Bar

A carpenter chiff-chaff is knock-nailing the notice of summer
    to the oaks,
a pair of tree-creepers toss a silver link of sound
from one to another,
and rococo wren-runs explode into trills.
On the headland, a pied flycatcher finds landfall from Africa,
shivers briefly on a post,
then darts after an English breakfast.

The asterisks of celandine drawing attention to spring
are the glossy gold of rank farmhouse butter
from childhood holidays,
pinned to the cowering turf by the gale
which snatches breath from the mouth,
then parts its fingers to let displaying daws
tumble and plummet through,
chacking their laughter;
which tacks a fulmar to the firmament,
buoys the broad brush-strokes of a buzzard,
exhales an exaltation of larks.

The ophiolitic birth of these stones
closed a sea-navel,
rumpled the Pennines;
they were poured out like psalmist's bones,
the phyllite sheen reflecting
an ancient crucible.
The ocean shades from grape-bloom horizon
to opalescent turquoise limen,
opposing moon-magnet and wind-wrack
shatter its glassy doom;
seethe-sucking the sterile shore dry,

the vehement undertow relinquishes no bodies,
its susurrating sibilance
ululating loss.

Clare Harding (SI Blackburn, England)

M 40

The motorway has slashed open the chalk,
still covertly signalled by tangles of Old Man's Beard,
the singular yellow of Field Maple,
while autumn smoulders.
With one eye on the road,
weaving through traffic,
I look for a reparative
Red Kite;
automatically discarding
the sable omens of corvid,
the languid sculling of grey gull,
the visual trill of a wind-hover,
till,
hanging by distant wing-tips
an archangel
plays with the air
ruddering the unique tail;
a pair execute a pas-de-deux
suspended above the scarp;
another, poised over the hard shoulder, talons stretched;
one planing down over woodland;
five, in total,
bless me on my journey.

Clare Harding (SI Blackburn, England)

SCOTLAND

Badenoch Waters

Grey mirror loch
wind-frowning
drowning
the ice-scoured strath;

leonine languorous lazing
over tawny serpentine sandbanks;

incisive steel
skinning schist and greywacke;

raven-dark pool
where gerrid wizards,
scurrying on hydrophobic thimbles,
scry out the secrets of souls;

each drop once
a grass-hung crystal of dew –
a tear on a distant lover's cheek.

Clare Harding (SI Blackburn, England)

The First of May
Duror, Morvern

First light:
along the ride
a dozen goldcrests
spin silver wheels of song.

The air is smudged
with the violet tread,
the rank ginger trail, of fox,
here stale
then pungent where he doubled back
later.

The imperious gait of a roe buck
follows the doe,
who splays wide ears,
then melts into the undergrowth.

From tiny twig chimneys
the larch flourishes sweep's brushes
of lime needles,
waiting for the sun to breathe
the coral embers of its flowers to life.

Clare Harding (SI Blackburn, England)

The Pattack

Snow
Sifts over larch-furred birch-burred slopes
Clots the stripling pine
Herring-bones a silver fir
Hunches over heath and heather;
The dipper-dunking river roars
Pours percussively
Over the roasted rib of magma
Plunges seething
Into iced peat-dark pools.
Boot-molars munch miles through it
White witness
Stag-slotted:
Rounding the hill, twenty-one
Bearing a ridiculous patrimony of antler
Balancing extravagant economies
Of grazing
Are caught in the spotlight.
Descending
Hare snow-shoed tracks,
Under the trees
A pair of roe have danced
Delicately in starlight.

Clare Harding (SI Blackburn, England)

Aoinheadh Mòr

The foresters' harvest massacred silence –
saws shrieked and whined,
a corduroy of alien conifer
groaned and crashed to fell, long-secret floors
gloom-mantled in needles,
where only toadstools had sucked sustenance
from darkness and decay;
logs rolled and rose,
brash barbered,
until light spilt on a deeper shame.

Fifteen families once hearthed here,
the cradling arms of the corrie
turning their faces to the sun
its loam-lap still marked by foxglove and meadow-sweet.
1824:
a few strokes of a distant pen
doomed a diaspora,
dispossession by an ovine tide.

A robin haunts the kailyards yet,
but the hammered percussion is the chack of a chat;
where children once toil-trundled boulders to clear the fields,
scarabs laboriously roll globes of marten dung;
the soft spun song of the women is only wind-whispered
where pipits parachute.
The burn mutters of the hissing of doused fires,
and rainbowed raindrops, hair-grass hung,
reflect the royal livery of flame that turned home to monument.
Pale bog-violets are the flowers of mourning,
And a lone Lorne loon laments.

Clare Harding (SI Blackburn, England)

Cairngorm

Weather has crumpled
granite into crumb,
glassy quartz and pink feldspar;
crouching behind boulders
tundra vegetation
clings doggedly to life,
each stalk skeleton icicle-coffined.
Wind has pleated the drifts,
polished banks of nevé to ice
under the burnishing sun.
The heft of ice-axe
initially unfamiliar
reawakens past rhythms
one – two – three – plant
boot slamming into blue shadow,
crust skittering down slopes
whispers histories.
Four thousand and eighty four feet
a personal Everest,
the summit clearly recalled
gloved hand on cairn.
The wind rips rents in the mist
letting the future
flood in.

Clare Harding (SI Blackburn, England)

SPAIN

I fell in love
'The Spanish Quartet' (February 2009)

I fell in love
With the warm Spanish sun
And the air like wine.
Orange and lemon trees,
Fountained squares,
Eyeline of mountains
Proud and strong.
Sound of church bells,
A century's prayers.

I fell in love
And was kissed and engulfed
In an Andalucian dream.
This was my Spain.
Not the tourist-filled costas,
Discos and bars.

Apart now, too long
The memories sweet
Remain a legacy
Time cannot erase.

I fell in love.

Jacque Emery (SI Canterbury, England)

Benahavis
'The Spanish Quartet' (February 2009)

Moorish citadel
on craggy peak,
Bastion outpost
 of a bygone age.
   Benahavis
Jumbled houses
 in ochre, white.
Brilliant, bright
with wrought-iron balconies.
   Benahavis
Bougainvillea
bursting forth
round window grilles
in shadowy squares.
   Benahavis
Delicate tiles
 of yellow and blue.
Patterned folklore
 on hill-steep streets.
   Benahavis
Crystal water,
spurting streams
 from fountainheads
of lions and dolphins.
   Benahavis
Suspended time
 on evening air.
Terrace dreams
 on wine warm skin.
   Benahavis.

Jacque Emery (SI Canterbury, England)

Watching the World

Skin like leather
Crumpled, brown.
Gap-toothed smiles,
Eyes bright as beams.
Twinkling friendship
In silent harmony.
Three men
Sitting
Watching the world.

Jacque Emery (SI Canterbury, England)

Flamenco
'The Spanish Quartet' (February 2009)

Still
Poised
Anticipating
Patrician profile
Head held high.
Pregnant
Perfumed
Sultry night
Waiting
Waiting
To begin.

Clap
Clap
Stamp
Clap clap
Stamp stamp
Palm on palm
Heel on heel

Flash of red
Swirl of shawl
Pounding feet
Pulsating sound.
Castanets
Like volleys of guns
Faster and faster
Guitar as drum.

Sight is sound
Sound is sight
Rhythmic fusion
Crescendoing life.

Jacque Emery (SI Canterbury, England)

SWITZERLAND

Mary Clarke *was born in Ashford, Kent, England. She qualified in Medicine from The Royal Free London in 1966 and, after some years in Occupational Health for British Rail, went into General Practice for 30 years, in a fairly deprived and multicultural practice in Croydon. In 1998 Mary re-qualified in Child Psychiatry at the Institute of Psychiatry. She retired from General Practice in 2002 and, since then, has been thoroughly enjoying her work with children with behavioural problems in Croydon. Mary's husband was a Graphic designer working for the Central Office of Information until 1993. They have 2 children – a daughter living in Switzerland with one daughter of her own, and a son in Oxford. Mary has been a member of SI Beckenham and District for over 20 years and has spent much of that time as recurrent Treasurer. She was President in 1994 and will be proposed as joint President again in 2010. In between work and Soroptimism, she enjoys gardening and renovating her small stone cottage in Normandie.*

Thoughts from Pilatus

A glimpse of dawn over ghostly mountains,
Pink tinged clouds glancing snow capped peaks,
Sparks of light catching dark blue waters,
Fleeting reminders of ancient worlds.

Crushing forces of age old mountains
Fiery boulders exploding skywards
Crashing to ground as blackening basalt
Casting new earth from destruction and hell.

Mammoth reflections of Shangri La
Mountainous beauty too vast to capture.
Ranges meeting in threatening landscape
Challenging man to strive and survive…

and

Crusty black mounds rising from oceans
Shaping new islands, dreaming of Eden,
Sand and shell crescents, azure blue waters
Creating new lands for all living things.

and

Savannah divided by Rift broadened valleys
Lifegiving lakes left as watery jewels.
Gentle green slopes where glaciers flowed
Forming pasture and dwelling for man and his herds.

This plentiful planet taking millions of years
To grow from the fire and explosion of suns
Has settled in orbit, protected by ozone,
Creating a world more precious than gold.

Mary Clarke (SI Beckenham and District, England)

TURKEY

Guzin Senbas *was born in Izmir, Turkey in 1934, and still lives in Izmir She worked for Turkish Telecommunications for many years but she is now retired. Guzin is a member of Izmir Soroptimist Club where she has held the offices of Secretary and Treasurer. Guzin likes writing poetry, reading books and handicrafts.*

A Story

I want to tell you a story,
If you'd lend me an ear.
Would you like to
Know about my country?

To its north is the Black Sea
Where anchovies dance with the waves
Young beauties clad in floral violet dresses
Pick hazelnuts; gather fresh tea leaves.

To the south rests the Mediterranean
Snow capped Taurus Mountains
Standing erect
Their cool plains refresh
In the heat of summer

In Konya, the golden wheat fields gently sway
Golden like the hair of my country's father, Atatürk, they shine.
Here rests Mevlana, a great thinker,
From his place of rest a thousand flutes sing his call
"Come! Come whoever you are,
Christian, Muslim, faiths of all kind…
Come again, whichever you are!"

Ankara stands joyful and proud
With the father of the nation in its arms
Who won an epic victory with his soldiers in Anafartalar
Never a warmonger,
He believed in 'Peace at home, Peace throughout the world'.
He rests in peace now,
As the leaders of the world salute him at the Mausoleum.

The 'Dadaş' of Erzurum,
Dance shoulder to shoulder,
Kneeing down and up so bold
Dancing happily the Turkish 'bar'
How proud of their country, they are.

My homeland, my Turkey,
Lies like a coy bride
All the way to Izmir of the Aegean Sea
Honey pours from the hives in the fields
Olive oil springs from the trees
Of this earth so fertile.

Look up to heaven
In Istanbul and Edirne,
The gems of Sinan, the architect.
Through my country passes
The historic Silk Road to connect
The land of Asia to Europe.

My crimson flag waves
Above my Turkey,
My Anatolia, my Home…
Flowing with respect and pride
To the world let our love be known.

Guzin Senbas (SI Izmir, Turkey)

BİR ÖYKÜ

Bir öykü anlatmak istiyorum
Sizlere dinlermisiniz?
Yaşadığım ülkeyi
Tanımak istermisiniz?
Yaşadığım ülke Türkiye
Kuzeyinde Karadeniz
Hamsiler dalgalarla dans eder,
Mor meneviş elbiseli güzel kızlarımız
Fındık Toplar. Çay derer.

Güneyde Akdeniz
Toroslar dimdik ayakta.
Başları karlı,
Yaz günlerinin sıcağında
Yurda hayat verir yaylaları.

Konya da nazlı nazlı sallanır
Buğday Başakları
Atasının saçlarından almış
Rengini sarımı, sarı.
Bir düşünür yatar orada
Mevlana Celalettin Rumi
Gel der, ne olursan ol
Yine gel, ister hırıstian
İster Müslüman.
Kim olursan ol, yine gel.
Sözlerini her an
Binlerce ney çalar.

Ankara Ata'sını almış
Kollarına çoşkuyla, gururla
Askerleriyle destan yazdı
Atatürküm Anafartalarda,
Asla savaşçı değildi.
Yurd da sulh, cihanda sulh

Olmuştu sloganı.
O yatıyor şimdi huzurla
Tüm Dünya liderleri
Selam duruyor ona Anıtkabirde.

Erzurum da dadaşlar,
Vermiş omuz omuza
Bar oynuyor, diz vuruyor,
Türk olmakla gurur duyuyor.

Nazlı bir gelin gibi
Uzanıyor Anayurdum, Türkiyem
Ege Denizi'ne, İzmir'e
Egenin dağından yağ,
Ovasından bal akar.
Yurduma bol bol bereket saçar.

İstanbul'da Edirne'de
Koca Sinanın yapıtları
Göklere bakar.
Tarihi ipek yolu boydan boya
Yurdumdan geçer,
Asya'yı Avrupa'ya bağlar.

Al bayrağım dalgalanır
Türkiye'min üzerinde
Anadolum, Türkiyem
Sevgi ile saygı ile
Dünya'ya kucak açar.

Guzin Senbas (SI Izmir, Turkey)

Imre Erten *was born in Konya, Turkey, in 1946 and graduated from İstanbul University, Faculty of Literature. She worked in several management units of the Ministry of Culture and retired in 2003. Imre is an artist, actress and poet. She has been a member of BUYAZ (Authors' Association of Bursa), UNIMA, Bursa Association Of Women Artists (she is the Acting President) and Uludag Soroptimist Club (Former President between 1999-2001). Imre has given 8 Personal and 60 Joint Exhibitions and has received several awards as an artist. She is also an amateur actress and has appeared in one part of a TV series called 'Yanik Koza' as a guest performer. Imre published her first poetry book 'Yalnizlik Ruzgari' in 1997 and 'Umut Denizi', the second, is about to be published. Imre is married to Op Dr Halil Erten and has one daughter.*

That's Ayvalik Here!

In the shore, smell of algae,
     My glass full of raki,
     On the table purslane with lemon,
     A plate of shrimp,
     Seabream, on the barbecue,
   Shiny phosphorescence
that reaches from Cunda to Ayvalik.
   Colorful lobsters sunbathing on the rocks,
   Boats line up on the shore bringing nets to the fishermen,
   South wind blows warmly,
   Cleans the lights of Midilli.
The sightseeing boats symbolize Ayvalık.
On the hill 'Seytan Sofrasi' (Devil's Table)
   People believed in the wish tree
they tied up the rags
   And murdered the nature,
   Murdered that beautiful peninsula.
   Cleaning comes from faith,

Environmentalism comes from people.
Let's get together for nature
    together, hand in hand …
With all creatures in Ayvalık,
To the most beautiful days of the future.

Iste Ayvalik Burasi

Kiyisinda yosun kokusu,
Kadehim raki dolusu,
Masamda limonlu semiz otu,
Bir tabakta karides,
Mangalda baliklardan isparoz,
Cunda'dan Ayvalik'a uzanan,
Kipir kipir yakamoz.
Kiyilara guneslemeye cikan,
Rengarenk istakoz.
Kiyilara dizilmisler,
Balikcilara ag tasiyan tekneler,
Ilik ilik esen guney ruzgari,
Midilli'nin isiklarini temizler.
Gezi motorlari ise Ayvalik'i simgeler.
Iste Ayvalik burasi.
Tepesinde Seytan Sofrasi.
Inanmislar dilek agacina,
Baglamislar pacavralari
Katletmisler dogayi.
O guzelim yarim adayi.
Temizlik imandan gelir,
Cevrecilik ise insandan.
Doga icin kenetlenelim
    Hep birlikte el ele …
Tum canlilarla Ayvalik'ta,
Yasanacak en guzel gunlere.

Imre Irten (SI Bursa Uludag, Turkey)
translated by Ece Sonmez

Bursa

Beautiful, lovable, historical Bursa
Entered my life with your green colour
With your arms surrounded old and new
Whoever sees you, cannot forget any longer.

Osman, Orhan, Emir Sultan, Asiyan
The curtains of Karagoz and Hacivat
The sound of the Sun, which never sinks
You are the symbol of the art, Bursa.

Silken scarves you have
You have snow on Uludag
Beloved ones in the hearts
You are the hope of the people, Bursa.

Plane trees reaching the sky
Boughs of chestnut, sweeter than honey
Places rooted in the past
You are the elixir of happiness, Bursa.

Hymns are told in your mystic nights
Gezeks are made in your houses
Getting sweetly drunk
In the bars of Arap Sukru.

My sweetheart with bridal dress
The sweetest ache in my tired heart
With the poem *Time in Bursa*, Bursa
You are my unforgettable love.

Imre Irten (SI Bursa Uludag, Turkey)
translated by Ece Sonmez

Bursa

Guzelsin, sirinsin, tarihsin Bursa
Yesilinle girdin dunyama,
Eski ile yeniyi saran kollarinla,
Seni goren, unutamaz bir daha.

Osman, Orhan, Emir Sultan, Asiyani
Karagoz ile Hacivat'ın perdesi
Batmayan Günes'in sesi ile
Sanatin simgesisin Bursa.

Ipekten sallarin var,
Uludag'da karlarin var,
Gonüllerde yarlarin var,
Insanların umudusun Bursa.

Bulutlara uzanan cinarlarinla,
Baldan tatli kestane dallarinla,
Gecmise kok salan mekanlarinla,
Mutluluk iksirisin Bursa.

Ilahiler soylenir mistik gecelerinde,
Gezekler yapilir hanelerinde,
Tatli bir sarhos olunur,
Arap Sukru meyhanelerinde.

Sen benim beyaz gelinlikli guzelim,
Yorgun kalbime düsen tatli sizimsin
Bursa'da zaman siirinle, Bursa,
Dillerden dusmeyen askimsin.

Imre Irten (SI Bursa Uludag, Turkey)
translated by Ece Sonmez

My World

I have a country
who turns green in the Middle East
Please
Don't lead it into a dead end with bitter games.

I have my people
who live in this land
Please
Don't deceive them with conspiracies.

I have a world
in which I live happily
Please
Don't take this away from me.

I have a character
That is a free spirit
Please
Don't silence this truth.

I have a life
which shoots out in nature
Please
Don't blacken it with fires.

I have a world
which rotates in art
Please
Don't stop it with politics.

Imre Irten (SI Bursa Uludag, Turkey)
translated by Ece Sonmez

Benim Dunyam

Bir ulkem var benim
Ortadogu'da yeseren,
Ne olur
Kotu oyunlarla cikmaza sokmayin.

Bir halkim var benim
Bu topraklarda yasayan
Ne olur
Entrikalarla kandirmayın.

Bir dunyam var benim
Mutlu yasadigim
Ne olur
Bu mutlulugu benden almayin.

Bir mizacim var benim
Firtinalar koparan
Ne olur
Bu firtinalara sebep olmayin.

Bir yasantim var benim
Dogada filizlenen
Ne olur
Yanginlarla karartmayin.

Bir dunyam var benim
Sanat icinde donen
Ne olur
Onu siyasetle durdurmayin.

Imre Irten (SI Bursa Uludag, Turkey)
translated by Ece Sonmez

THE UNITED STATES OF AMERICA

Kathy McElvany *was born in Kansas City, Missouri, USA, but she has lived for most of her life in Upland, California at the base of the San Gabriel Mountains. Kathy married her High School sweetheart. They have two children, three grandsons and one granddaughter. Kathy is a certified travel and cruise consultant and has owned two travel agencies. She now enjoys working from home and when she's not travelling (she has been to every continent in the world) Kathy is busy working in her garden, reading, going to the movies with friends or just enjoying life with her family. She is also the vice-chairwoman of her County Jails Commission and is an honorary deputy sheriff with the County. Kathy also shoots Trap & Skeet on the San Bernardino County Sheriff's Trap & Skeet Team. Both Kathy and her husband had mothers who were in the same Soroptimist club together! Kathy has been a Soroptimist for 23 years and has been president of two different clubs. She is currently the Golden West Region SI Liaison Officer and tries very hard to help clubs understand the importance of the international connections. Kathy has represented SI of the Americas as a speaker in Vienna for a workshop on the Transnational Crime of Trafficking in Human Beings. She has also spoken in Beijing, at the 'All Chinese Women's Association' and in Shanghai at the 'Shanghai Women's Association'. Kathy has served on the Golden West Region Board as a district director, treasurer and governor-elect. She had to resign from the last position, however, due to surgery that went wrong, leaving her with much-reduced eyesight and short-term memory loss. Kathy believes that this period of her life taught her to value her true friends. She also believes that being a member of Soroptimist International is one of the most important things in her life!*

My Home

The morning sun shines through my window and I am blessed
with a feeling of peace.

The camellias are in full bloom now and their vibrant colors
make me smile and want to reach through the window
and take them to my senses. There is still a small bird's nest
in one of the plants, abandoned by last year's occupants. I
wonder if these same parents will remember the safety they
enjoyed and return again this year?

Myriad of greens set majestically at the base of our powerful
San Gabriel Mountain range. I look at the snow-capped
peaks of Mount Baldy and Cucamonga Peak and know that
another progression of seasons is prospering.

A ring-neck dove takes flight from our giant redwood tree with
no care more than landing on yet another sunny branch to
rest.

The rains have subsided, though we have not had hard rain
since last month. Gentle rain makes me all the more ready
to plan my spring garden and turn over the good earth
to prepare for planting of vibrant flowers and healthy
vegetables to be enjoyed in the months to come.

Walking my small dog up the canyon of the mountains this
morning, we saw two coyotes. They are not a threat now, but
they will be mating soon and once their pups are whelped,
both mother and father will be hunting furiously to feed
them. Then, my small dog will need to be held more closely
to home. His playtime in our peaceful backyard overlooking
the valley will need to be chaperoned. We can't blame the
coyotes for trying to provide for their children, any more
than we would do what we must, to provide for our own.
We have encroached upon their territory and their sphere of

hunting is reduced year after year as homes are built further
and further into *their* hunting grounds.

The oranges and tangerines are ripe for picking today and I'm
hoping to gleam as many as possible to take to our local
women's shelters. It is always my pleasure to watch the fruits
of my labor bloom and prosper and with God's help be able
to pass on nourishment to those in need. Peace abounds and
life is good!

Kathy McElvany (SI of the Foothills, California, USA)

Irene Morris *was born in Chicago, Illinois, USA in 1920. Her
family moved to California in 1937. When the Second World
War began, Irene worked as a final inspector of parachutes
for the Armed Forces. She married in 1945, has 3 children, 3
grandchildren and 5 great-grandchildren. In 1975 her family
moved to South Lake Tahoe, California. Irene's husband was a
general building contractor for 54 years and she was co-owner
and office manager for Morris Buildings. Irene was President of
the Business and Professional Women's Club and has received
the Woman of the Year Award. She has worked tirelessly for a
number of voluntary organizations. Irene has attended church all
her life and served as the Luther League Advisor for 20 years. She
has also been a Sunday School teacher and a Girl Scout Leader.
Irene was a Barton Hospital Auxiliary member for over 20
years, working in the hospital gift shop. Irene joined Soroptimist
International of Tahoe Sierra as a Charter Member in 1977, was
President in 1982-1983 and has been made a Life Member.*

My World

My world is just a small speck,
when sitting on my fabulous deck.
The beautiful river is gently flowing by,
while ducks fly high in the sky.

Soft white clouds form below the pale blue sky,
breathless to see our eagles soaring high.
Love opens my world wide, while giving service
with great pride. Soroptimist spreading seeds,
to help the world in need.
We clasp hands around the world,
say our pledge, we are together,
working in all kinds of weather.
Knowing we will always be together forever,
for country and for God.

Irene Morris (SI Tahoe Sierra, California, USA)

Deborah Stojevich *was born and raised in Minneapolis, Minnesota, USA. She now lives in Kingman, Arizona. She is a landlord and works in Real Estate. Deborah has been married for 23 years and has 2 stepsons and 2 granddaughters. She joined Soroptimist International of Kingman in 2003. Deborah was the club Recording Secretary for two years and is currently the SoroptiNEWS letter editor, a post she has held for the last four years!*

The Swamp Next Door

Shoreless and vast,
The soft glass surface
Disguises the depth.

Murky tendrils, wait below.
Shift in sediment, bide their time.
Should I venture in too far,
Slimy shadows with loving arms
Will grab and pull me under.
Smother my breath with bottomless affection.

Smells of death and decomposition
Warn me not to become too friendly.

Yet still there is life.

Hidden within the cattails,
An unseen bird calls.
A turtle pokes its head above the skin.
Sunlight peaks through leaves,
Cavorts with the skittish multitude,
Dances upon the surface.

A foolish child, I creep closer still.
Attracted like those that crawl, fly and slither
To skim, slide and glide upon the surface.
To observe or feed at the edge.

Drawn to the life that surrounds and abounds
In the dark, murky water.

Deborah Stojevich (SI Kingman, Arizona, USA)

Florence S. Evans *was born in New Salem, Pennsylvania, USA,*
and moved to Bridgeton, New Jersey when she got married.
She has been retired for five years from Cumberland County
Government where she worked for thirty years and was the
Deputy Surrogate. Florence enjoyed her job immensely. It
was centered in Family Court and consisted of dealing with
the probate of wills, estate work and the adoption of children.
Florence has been a member of Soroptimist International of
Cumberland County for 26 years and was President from 1987-
1989. She also served on the Board of Directors. Florence says
that she is proud and happy to be a Soroptimist. She has been
married to Norman for 53 years and has two children and two
grandchildren. They also have a dog, Cassie, a Jack Russell. In
her retirement Florence enjoys reading since there wasn't time
while she worked! Her main interest is history.

Haiku

The hard brown earth cracks.
   From a bulb deep in the ground
      a crocus is born.

Apprehensively,
   a wide-eyed child surrenders
      to her first haircut.

Warm sun, mild breezes,
   green leaves peeking through the ground.
      Mother Nature's gift.

Florence S Evans (SI Cumberland County, New Jersey, USA)

Sharon Lenahan *is 64 years old and lives in Red Bluff, Northern California, USA. She attended university in Chico, California and her degrees are in criminal justice and psychology. She continued her education with numerous other classes, including law school and is now a licensed private investigator as well as being a deputy probation officer. Sharon works with juveniles who are wards of the court and need group home placement. Many of them belong to criminal street gangs, and this was the inspiration for her poem, ' Gang Banging'. She travels all over the state of California and occasionally out of state for her employment. Most of the time the job is rewarding. Sharon is married and has one daughter who has three boys. She also has two stepsons and has 5 grandchildren from them! Her husband is retired and helps her at home. Sharon belongs to SI Red Bluff, in the Sierra Nevada Region of the Americas. She enjoys being a Soroptimist and being able to attend the conferences, especially the award ceremonies.*

Gang Banging

Surenos are blue,
flashing signs, throwing thirteens,
South of Bakersfield.

Nortenos are red,
flashing signs, throwing fourteens,
North of Bakersfield.

Males, females alike,
jumped in, jumped out, they still fight;
threats, violence, and murder.

Illicit drug sales,
monikers and graffiti

and drive-by shootings.

And related crimes
racially motivated,
street terrorism.

In California
Crips, Bloods, Skinheads, Peckerwoods;
hate crimes, fear and force.

Hate crimes, terror times.

Sharon Lenahan (SI Red Bluff, California, USA)

Gloria Hill *was born in Burbank, California, USA and has
lived most of her life in Southern California. She moved to Palm
Springs and started her own tax and accounting business. She
is married and has 4 sons and 5 grandchildren. She became a
Soroptimist in 1992, and has served as President of SI Palm
Desert-Sunrise. In 2002 Gloria helped to charter a new club and
she is now a charter member of SI Palm Springs. She has served
on the Soroptimist Golden West Region board of directors for
the last nine years, and been District Director, Treasurer, and
currently Governor-elect. From 1998-2001 Gloria served on
the Palm Springs Human Rights Commission, requiring her to
oversee activities, write the annual report that was distributed
to the City Council, and help coordinate public forums relating
to human rights issues. Gloria believes that this was because
of her involvement in an organization that advocates and
promotes human rights for women. During her tenure they were
instrumental in bringing about the televising of Soroptimist
meetings and forums on public access television, which gave
the club more visibility in the community. Gloria has also
been a member of the Work Advisory Committee for her local
community college for 8 years and has been successful in hiring*

and training 3 different women in her Accountancy Practice.
In her spare time, Gloria loves to write poetry and she has been
published several times. She enjoys travelling and attending
Soroptimist meetings and events. Aside from her family, Gloria
says that she counts her Soroptimist membership as one of the
best things that has ever happened to her!

And I'll Pass My Days Remembering

The deep blue skies and white puffy clouds
Welcome the perfect day.
The sound of birds chirping and the smell of fresh air
Bring peace and tranquility my way.

The flowers burst with color, their aroma delights the senses,
While children laugh and play, behind their picket fences.

The tall majestic mountains stand silently in their place,
With deep mosaic shadows streaking through the mountain's
    face.

My heart leaps with joy and my senses remain alert,
As I treasure the fleeting moment, the way I would savor a fine
    dessert.

And I'll pass my days remembering the times that I stood
    there,
When my eyes no longer focus and my body is beyond repair,

The beauty that I'll remember will stay vivid in my mind,
Until my God does call me, until the end of time.

Gloria Jean Hill (SI Palm Springs, California, USA)

OUR THOUGHTS

THE EARTH – THE ENVIRONMENT – NATURE

Audrey Harper *emigrated from the UK to New Zealand in 1953 and taught at secondary school level until retirement in 1981. She was a charter member of SI Upper Hutt, in 1975 and has served the club as Secretary and President. Audrey is still busy: with voluntary library work, woolcraft in a variety of forms, travelling (when she can afford it), writing short stories and poetry, tutoring adult groups to encourage recording of personal memories, and Tai Chi. A very busy and rewarding working life and retirement!*

Planet Earth

Our world,
far from distant planets
Our sun,
lighting our darkness
Our earth
full of beauty and richness
Our people,
men, women and children
Our struggle,
justice and peace for all
Our task,
help where needed
Our gifts,
shared freely with others
Our hope,
a wonderful world.

Audrey Harper (SI Upper Hutt, New Zealand)

"Let there be light"

And God said
"Let there be light"
and there was –
so he decorated the heavens
with a sun and some stars –
he didn't make a moon
because he hadn't invented night
and then he made a hedgehog.
This is great fun, he thought,
and he made some deer
and an elephant
and a rhino
and slipped fish into the sea
and laughed as he fitted
eight tentacles onto an octopus.
Only then did he think of night
and a luminous moon.
And then he made a mistake –
he invented man
and from his rib –
why?
God only knows –
a woman and a serpent
and apples
and trees of life.
Then a whole bunch of jealous and stupid
creatures were born
who destroyed the trees
and hunted the animals
and finally
each other.
And God thought,
"Although they've reached the heights
of genius
and the depths of depravity

I haven't taken into consideration
that they only use 6% of their brains.
I'll have to make a plan
but I'm so tired I'm going to sleep
for 3 million years
and when I wake up
perhaps they will have evolved
and taken control
of the universe."
So God yawned and turned over
and when he awoke
there was nothing left –
except night and day
and the sun and the stars
and the moon
and a scorched earth
and an angry sea
and no life –
whatsoever.

Hannah Lurie (SI Durban, South Africa)

Olwen Jones *was born in Derby, England, 76 years ago. She eventually settled in Bootle, Merseyside where, having worked in Derby, London and North Wales as an Architectural Assistant, she qualified as a Technician. Olwen married in 1966 and took a position as a Technical Librarian which she held for 6 years. Her return to the drawing board brought her success and encouraged her to found her own practice. This prospered initially, but eventually she had to abandon it after a series of family illnesses culminating, in late 1980, with Olwen herself suffering a cerebral haemorrhage. Through the 1980s she secured further qualifications, struggled to find work and became a Soroptimist. A member of SI Bootle, she captained the Bowls team for several years. On retiring, Olwen cared for her mother in her last years and worked in the voluntary sector. Last year Olwen was elected to the Board of Governors at Aintree University Hospital's NHS Foundation Trust.*

The End days?

The plates of the Earth are moving, grinding,
All the icebergs are melting, at both poles.
  So where is all the ice-water going?
Is this why land loss is not leaving holes?
Furthermore the continents move northward,
  Antarctica will be habitable (?)
But will it be soon enough, does time afford?
  Will land then appear, be available?
Seems we proceed in a manner that's blind,
  Being not at all sure of the causes.
Does what man does really compound in kind
Damage the Earth wields from its resources?
  Yet could it simply be that in its run
The Earth wobbled, and is nearer the sun?

Olwen Jones (SI Bootle, England)

Sheila Eustace, *born in 1932, was married and has two children. She had a long career in publicity management handling advertising, PR and exhibitions, working for international companies operating in the building/engineering industry. In the last years of her working life she managed a business centre in Croydon. Sheila has been a member of SI Croydon for 21 years and during this time has been both Secretary and President. She is a very committed Soroptimist and has regularly attended Region meetings, SIGBI conferences and International conventions. She has travelled extensively, mainly back-packing, meeting up with Soroptimists worldwide, and only ill-health has prevented her from continuing these travels after 2003. Sheila is currently Chairman/ Director of a freehold company. She has sometimes been asked to write poetry for special events. The following poem was written for the inaugural supper of President Patricia Painting, SI Croydon and District, UK, 12 May 2005.*

Painting the Town Green

The environment, our chosen project
An infinite and wide-ranging subject
With so many issues that do affect
All our lives

Climate change is so complex
With dried up rivers and lakes
Yet icebergs melt and rivers flood
It seems a contradiction

Recycling is the mantra of today
But during the war we used to say
Make do and mend, it had to be that way
We've gone full circle

So how do we make the young aware
When they shop till they drop without a care
It's a daunting task when not based on need
In this throwaway society

Though air is cleaner and there's little fog
No open fires and hence no smog
But what about all the cars that clog
Polluting the atmosphere

Fairtrade is important for African dignity
But only charity's offered, causing dependency
EU trading rules just ruin their economy
Protectionism prevails

Bitterly cold winters are now in the past
Ice and snow no longer last
Plants are blooming all year round
What on earth is happening?

Water Aid is an ongoing theme
Forming part of an overall scheme
Something we westerners take for granted
Because it's always there

We leave taps running needlessly
Without a thought of scarcity
And never consider how it must be
In the third world
A pot on your head, a long walk from the well
Imagine the horror when you tripped and fell
And have to go back and do it again
Must be sheer hell

So as our interest and concern progresses
We'll learn more of the strains and stresses
To get people to save the planet's resources

For future generations

Tomorrow we can all paint the town green
But for tonight let's just set the scene
Please charge your glasses, (and water will do)
To welcome our president, not one recycled
But one who is bright and shiny and new.

Sheila Eustace (SI Croydon and District, England)

Blackthorn at Easter

From tortured thorns
from bare black bones
burst out
minute crimson chalices
cupping pentamerous petals
a million-fold
wreathing a wraith-breath of blossom

A perfidy of pollen
calculated tiny cruelties
turn into fruit frosted with the patina
of watched cold-blue dawns
into sloe-dark boughs

The sour harvest
sucks speech from the mouth

Clare Harding (SI Blackburn, England)

Ownership

We bought our house and garden plot
 Over twenty years ago,
We paid our mortgage on the dot
 And felt we owned this sacred spot,
Alas, we find that we do not.

The garden is the battleground,
 So many owners in competition,
Hardcased beasties, fur and feather
 Trees and flowers conspire together
To claim for each a treasured spot
 Do we own it? We do not!

Cats have commandeered the lot,
 Claimed it as their own domain.
Two patrol the territory,
 King for the moment, alert and wary,
Fearful of banishment from this spot,
 Recapture from cats? We would rather not!

Foxes make it their motorway
 A convenient route from A to B.
Field mice travel on shorter legs,
 Badgers once and fuzzypegs,
Cutting a road through this local spot,
 Compulsory purchase? We regret not!

Birds in flocks come flying down
 To meet, to feed, to strut around,
Starlings, Sparrows, Dunnocks, Jays,
 Blackbirds, Thrushes, come and stay.
The Robin reigns upon this plot
 He is the monarch. We are not!

Squirrels shop in the superstore
 Choice of nut and seeds galore.
Abseiling down with effortless pull
 Defying gravity they stuff themselves full.
Storing for winter in this neighbourly spot
 A money spinner? Surprisingly not!

Trees and plants mature in season
 Sink deep roots and bask in the sun.
The ancient Iris stand pranked and tall
 While apples ripen and gently fall,
Year on year they remain in this spot
Will we outstay them? I think not!

What shall we do with these marauders?
 Battle the hatches? Repel the borders?
Take them to court to claim possession?
 No judge would grant me such a concession,
Just for the sake of a garden plot
 Oh certainly not! Certainly not!

So how do we feel who linger here?
 Cutting the grass, tending the banks,
Willingly, lovingly, regardless of thanks.
 We have learned that if you stand and stare
Or sit relaxed in garden chair,
 You can catch an echo as light as air
"You have your share. You have your share."

Su Rennison (SI Canterbury, England)

Linda Beddows *was born in Salford, England in 1954. The family moved to Lytham St Annes, Lancashire,when she was 10 and she has lived there ever since. In fact, she is now living in the same road they moved to some 44 years ago. Linda enjoyed her teenage years at Queen Mary School, Lytham and she is now a Governor there. Linda took Business Studies at college which she combined with a secretarial course. Her career since then has taken several paths, working firstly for an estate agent then with quantity surveyors (a somewhat mad and enjoyable existence!); followed by 26 years as a Recruitment Consultant with a local firm where she eventually became Managing Director and part-owner. Linda is now semi-retired and works as a consultant. She also qualified as a teacher in commercial subjects and taught both word processing and shorthand at a college for adult education; obtained a TESOL qualification for teaching English as a foreign language; became a Fellow of the Recruitment Employment Federation and a Fellow of the Royal Society of Arts. She is married to David,, a very patient and understanding 'Soroptimister'. Linda has been a Soroptimist for 15 years and in that time has been Club President and,last year, Regional President of NW England and the Isle of Man. She is very active in her local community being Chair of the local League of Hospital Friends, and a Trustee at the Trinity Hospice in Bispham. She also does the administration for the local Child Contact Centre. Linda is currently undertaking a Diploma in Life Coaching. Linda loves languages and is fluent in Spanish. Her interests include literature, travel, theatre, food, dancing, seeing their friends and walking – not necessarily in that order!*

Beauty

Beauty is many different things
    The crystal teardrop on a spider's web
    The lithe lean limbs of a tiger
    The deep blue sea off a far away isle
    The pure white drift of snow
Beauty is many different things, as we have come to know!

Beauty is many different things
    The sleeping pup by its mother's side
    The lightning flash in a storm
    The wonderful glow of the Northern Lights
    The dark grey winter sky
Beauty is many different things, as time passes us by!

Beauty is many different things
    The rainbow following the heavy rain
    The bird in flight on high
    The bright balloon on a summer's day
    The baby's very first smile
Beauty is many different things, and surrounds us all the while!

Linda Beddows (SI The Fylde, England)

The Swan

Seemingly motionless as we went by,
She was gliding – the action all below.
Her charges, who before had been busy,
Now were taking refuge from the stream's flow,
Snuggled beneath her wings, their safety sure.
She was alert, watching for signs of her prey,
To feed her brood she needed fodder, pure,
So they would be strong when they flew away.
Thus watching and guiding, healing their hurt,
They grow, she lets them explore, even stray.
From her experience, direction sought
Takes them on their first migration away.
The weak stay close, they could always belong,
All tenderly nurtured: most will grow strong.

Olwen Jones (SI Bootle, England)

Anne Pickup *was born in Blackburn (Lancashire, England) 68 years ago and she still lives there! She is now retired but worked for many years in the National Health Service as an Orthoptist. Anne is a Trustee of the charity Friends of Chernobyl's Children (UK) which was started in Blackburn. Her interests include playing the piano, running the Church choir, and being an accompanist for other organisations. She is married to David and they recently celebrated their Ruby Wedding. Anne has two small grandsons and they keep her very busy! She has been a Soroptomist for over ten years and has enjoyed every moment.*

Silence

Is silence a reality –
Does it really happen?
Does the baby in the silent womb
Hear its mother's heart beat?
Do we consider the silence
When the children are asleep?
Or when we sit beside a river deep
And hear it gurgle and plunge to hidden depths
Where maybe silence lies.
Do we know silence in the deepest rural fields?
Or do we hear the Lark's high call
As she soars into her own silent skies?
Do we know silence when we sit without a word?
Do we hear the breathing of those around us
And do we really care?
The silence of the World is maybe when
We do not hear the call of those in despair –
The sick, the dying, the abused, the forgotten
Who in their silent world cry out for a listening ear
And ask us "Are you there?"
Is silence a reality –
Does it really happen?

Anne Pickup (SI Blackburn, England)

FRIENDSHIP – RELATIONSHIPS – LOVE

Wendy Grimshaw *was born in Blackpool, England and has lived there for 63 years. She ran a family owned bathroom showroom until three years ago when she retired. Wendy is in the Salvation Army and now helps to run the community care side of the Army. She has four grandchildren and two great granddaughters, Her son and grandsons do motorbike scrambling and, as Wendy is a Marshall, she finds herself in a field many weekends. Wendy has been a Soroptimist for 6 years and in that time she has held the offices of Secretary, then President, and Secretary once again!*

Our Soroptimist Friendship

We meet in fellowship, friends together,
We have days out – a get-together,
We never mind whatever the weather,
We're friends together.

We laugh a lot – have fun together,
Share sorrows and joys – support one another,
We give of our best to help sisters and brothers,
New friends to gather.

We meet for a coffee – the time doesn't matter,
We sit and we talk – have a good natter,
But in our enjoyment of sharing the patter,
We'll talk about things that are important – that matter.

There are things in the world that need all our attention,

Places where sisters live under great tension,
Women and children who need all our devotion,
To doing good deeds.

So whilst we enjoy all the fun and the laughter,
We think about things that our efforts might alter,
And I trust that our care and concern never falters,
We're SOROPTIMISTS together.

Wendy Grimshaw (SI The Fylde, England)

Oh no, not again!

You will remember the beautiful dish,
The Optician, I know you enjoyed him.
It happened again; by no means my wish,
Someone of interest got under my skin.
I'm not saying who, did not pitch a woo.
Was tempted, saw reason, would not be rash.
So what could I do; it just wasn't true
That I in a flash could cut quite a dash.
It's good after all that I can still fall,
My bones may be old but my heart's not cold,
And beauty portrayed can make us all tall.
Should faint hearts revive, can we yet be bold?
Oh well, maybe not, I'll keep my cool,
Yes, consider my years, make it a rule.

Olwen Jones (SI Bootle, England)

Bernadette Archuleta *was born in Colorado, USA. She has lived in Southern California for the last 19 years, the past 11 being in Corona. She began her career in publishing until she changed to the field of Business Services. She is currently an Account Executive with Payday Payroll Service, having worked for them for 8 years. Bernadette is a very new Soroptimist and is impressed with her club, SI Corona and the mission of Soroptimists around the world. She likes to spend her time cooking, gardening, reading and making up stories. She loves to travel and has been to 4 of the top beaches in the world! Bernadette has a 5 year old daughter, an amazing family and loyal friends. She feels that no matter what trials she has faced, she has felt loved and supported. These are the people who inspire her poetry, and she dedicates her work to them.*

Love's Journey

I've been blessed to see many degrees of love
To be born and raised with the deepest of love
Unconditional, overflowing, ever growing love

There are no limits on its gifts, freely given love
I've seen it taken and neglected, unappreciated love
It heals and mends and keeps together, the forgiveness of love

A life with love is full and strong and keeps us going on.

Bernadette M Archuleta (SI Corona, California, USA)

Sue Berry *is a retired Primary School teacher. She has lived in the same house in Crawley Down, West Sussex, England, for the last 32 years. Before that she moved a great deal including spending two years in Houston, Texas, USA. She has two sons, one born in Texas, and two grandchildren. Her husband is also retired so they have now started travelling again – but this time for pleasure. Sue joined Soroptimist International of East Grinstead in 1994 and was Club President, for the first time, 1998-1999. In 2002 following the sad death of Liz Sandwell (a much loved member who was due to be President for her club's 40th anniversary), Sue joined with two other members to take on the Presidency for that year as well. She is a keen painter and it was through her love of painting that she met the subject of her poem. She also enjoys reading poetry but this is her first attempt to write any.*

Watching Her Die

She was a mother figure, a friend and a teacher.

Watching her die brought the memories flooding back.

She was a humanist and a lover of all life.

Watching her die made the past the present.

She was an atheist who was truly religious.

Watching her die was a lesson in courage.

She was my friend and I was privileged to know her.

Watching her die showed me the wonder of living.

Sue Berry (SI East Grinstead, England)

Ruth Puddick *was born in Chichester, England in 1945 and educated in Cambridge. She joined Barclays Bank in the 60s and became a Foreign Exchange specialist. In 1977, after the Equal Opportunities Act came into being, she joined the Institute of Bankers, qualified in 1980 and was made a Fellow in 1992. Widowed at an early age, with no children, Ruth was the first female Bank Manager appointed by Barclays in East Anglia. Retiring in 1993 due to chronic Rheumatoid Arthritis, she acted as a consultant to St. John's Innovation Centre, working on local and Government financed projects to help small technology businesses. She also found time to serve on 3 housing associations, The Prince's Trust and more recently has been a Trustee of an Independent Sixth Form College. Ruth joined Soroptimist International of Cambridge in 1986 and served as Hon. Treasurer for two years. Infirmity precludes her from attending many meetings but she keeps in contact with club members by email and the occasional Dinner. Current interests include cruising, listening to music, good literature, following sport and keeping contact with her Bank customers, many of whom are firm friends! Her poem, 'Remembrance', was written for an elderly man she befriended who had been in Bomber Command in the RAF during World War 2. Many of his friends had died and, every year (even with Parkinsons) he went to the War Memorial and stood in the cold to honour old comrades. Ruth and her friend used to send each other poems, usually funny ones, but one year the local paper took a photograph of him and he sent her a copy. It was then that she wrote the poem. He used to have it framed with the photo and it hung on his wall until he died, when it was returned to her.*

Remembrance

There stand the gallant warriors bold,
Braving November's wind and cold,

Remembering fallen friends and foe
Who fought and died, so long ago.
Their faces wet with mist and tears
As they recall those war-torn years,
When young at heart and brave and true,
They risked their lives for me, and you.

Their fallen comrades they remember
On the eleventh of each November,
Lives lost on land, in sea and air
Many perished and they know not where.
A two minute silence for quiet prayer,
To show the world that they still care,
Laying a wreath with a trembling hand
Is an action seen across the land.

But they knew those comrades cared
That their loved ones should be spared,
And offered up their lives that we
Should live in peace, indefinitely.
And as they honour those who died
With tear filled eyes they cannot hide,
Recalling some who shed their blood
At Gallipoli and in Flanders mud.

Perhaps later conflicts cause the pain
With memories of El Alamein
No matter where, the price is high
Whenever comrades fall and die.
So spare a thought for those warriors bold
Standing so silent, proud and cold,
Remembering those who paid the price
And made the greatest sacrifice.

Ruth Puddick (SI Cambridge, England)

Poco Davis *was born and raised in Winnipeg,
Manitoba,Canada. She was adopted at an early age and has had
the pleasure of meeting her biological mother and discovering
her three sisters and brother. She was married and has a son and
two grandsons. Poco lived in Reno, Nevada, USA for 15 years
and then moved to Las Vegas, where she has spent the last 22
years. She is a Licenced Drug and Alcohol Counselor. Poco has
been a Soroptimist for 27 years. She has been President of two
different clubs, served on region committees and is currently the
Immediate Past Governor of the Sierra Nevada Region. Poco has
attended several international conferences and SIA conventions.
She loves every minute of the service mission of Soroptimism.
Living in Winnipeg, Poco became an avid curler and enjoyed the
sport for the early part of her life. She also plays golf and tennis,
loves to hike and write poetry.*

Relationships

Whether it be a significant other, a friend, family or co-worker
What makes the difference, well, in reality nothing.
When we look at what it really is, it is all the same.
We love unconditionally
We seek intimacy and we trust.
We think out of the box and dream together.
The other is the most important
not me.

We do not seek to please but to seek pleasure
We speak not to be right but to discover
We listen not to be polite but to engage
We trust not to get something from it but to love and be loved

It is not a game
not who is right or who is wrong
but a commitment
To be there, always and to want to be there for each other.

It is a gift to have a relationship with another human being, not
   a given.

Why do we not appreciate the little, most wonderful times,
but feel instead, that we must have the best,
the most perfect and not the least, what we do not deserve.

To have this wonderful energy and feel the love we must work
   but not work as an ordeal
but instead as a gift we give one another.

Poco Davis (SI Metro Las Vegas, Nevada, USA)

At The Supermarket

As I hand picked the pears
the Fijian lass sweeping the floor
leant on her broom

"My problem is I'm 17
My dad has my husband picked out
it's his best friend's son"

"I don't know him
I want to live alone
and get on with my life"

"It's so hard
all the arrangements are made
my father will be so happy"

You want to handpick your husband
as I choose pears
I understand

Frances Meech (SI Wellington, New Zealand)

Gisela Hertel *was born in 1936 in Nürnberg, Frankonia, Germany. She is married and has one daughter. Gisela is now retired but she was a pharmacist. She has lived in Palatinate near Mannheim, Heidelberg and Baden-Baden. Gisela is an active Soroptimist and is a member of SI Frankenthal. She has responsibility for health-care and environmental issues in the club and is currently President.Gisela is also a member of a culture club in Steinbach-Baden-Baden. She loves to write poems and short stories and often takes part in public readings in hospitals and other public institutions. Gisela also likes photography,travel, reading and sport – especially tennis, walking and swimming.*

Together

I can't pick specks of dust from your path,
or weave you a mantle of stars.
I can't prevent you from weeping at times,
when your courage retreats behind bars.

I can't stitch you a shielding suit
to ward off the harsh jolts of fate.
I can't prevent you from vowing at times,
"Its over. For ever. Too late."

Yet, I can offer my aid, my strength, love and time.
We could hammer our plans, be armed against wrong.
So let's work together in this fickle life,
then we, you and me, we will stand strong.

Gisela Hertel (SI Frankenthal, Germany)
translated by Gwendolen Webster (SI Aachen, Germany)

Gemeinsam

Ich kann Dir nicht jedes Staubkorn von Deinem Lebensweg
    picken
und ich kann Dir keinen Sternenmantel weben.
Ich kann Dir keinen Schutzanzug stricken,
der Dich bewahrt vor den Schicksalsschlägen im Leben.

Ich kann nicht verhindern, dass Du ab und zu weinst,
wenn die Verzweiflung stärker ist als der Mut.
Ich kann nicht verhindern wenn Du ab und zu meinst:
"Alles ist aus und nichts wird mehr gut."

Aber ich kann Dir meine Hilfe anbieten,
meine Kraft, meine Liebe und meine Zeit,
wir könnten gemeinsam Pläne schmeiden
und wären besser gegen die Risiken des Lebens gefeit.

Ich kann Dir nicht jedes Staubkorn von Deinem Lebensweg
    picken
und ich kann Dir keinen Sternenmantel weben,
doch wenn wir gemeinsam in eine Richtung blicken,
dann sind wir stark in diesem so wankelmütigen Leben.

Gisela Hertel (SI Frankenthal, Germany)

---

*Ashlee Austin was born in 1984 in Bridgeton, New Jersey, USA.
She now lives in Vineland, New Jersey – but aspires to live in
Las Vegas one day! She graduated from Rowan University in
2006 with a degree in Communications (Radio, TV and film)
and currently works with her mother full-time as an Insurance
Agent. Her mother, Paula, has been a Soroptimist since 1991 and
is a member of SI Cumberland County. She is currently North
Atlantic Region District 11 Director and Past President, and has
also been on the Board of Directors. Ashlee has been involved*

*in numerous Soroptimist events with Paula, such as helping
with yard sales, Santa lunches, Peach Festivals and many more
activities. She plans to become a fully committed Soroptimist
when she has settled on her career and place of residence. Ashlee
is single. She loves music, art and poetry and is an avid reader.
She loves to travel and go to Broadway plays and musicals.*

Love (d)

The man I loved no longer exists –
He withered and faded away.
The man I loved is gone forever-
Leaving me in disarray.
What remains is so little
Memories and pictures
And a lingering feeling-
Of loss.
No date on a headstone
Where 'we' became 'me' –
Nowhere to mourn the death
Of 'us'.
His voice is the ghost
Of a long dead lover –
Though it sounds the same.
His face is the shadow
Of a fading image –
With whom he shares a name.
The man I loved
Fell in love with
Someone else.
The man I loved
Fell in love
With a stranger – himself.

Ashlee Austin (Paula Austin, SI Cumberland County,
New Jersey, USA)

Major Jeri Bawden *served with her late husband Major*
George Bawden for more than 40 years in The Salvation Army,
ministering in Churches and also working with drug and alcohol
addicted men. They served in many parts of California until
finally escaping to the beautiful state of Washington, USA, on
the Olympic Peninsula. As the gateway to Victoria, Canada,
Jeri loves to travel across the Straight to that beautiful city. Jeri
learned about Soroptimism when she was 14 years old from
her officer at the Salvation Army. It took another 14 years until
she was finally able to have the great joy of joining in Anaheim,
California in 1968. She has served as President of two clubs:
Stockton, California and Port Angeles, Washington. She also
served as District I Secretary and then District I Director in
the Northwestern Region of Soroptimist International of the
Americas. She has been writing poems and songs since she was a
child, has three self-published books and has won several poetry
awards.

Teamwork

Into the air on massive wings
the glorious eagle flies,
she swoops and swirls and circles low
then soars into the skies.
Alone, upon the current
majestic to behold
she needs no help, she leads the way,
so beautiful – so bold!

Across the sky the geese appear
they fly in perfect rhythm,
their special sound a signal
that all should watch the heavens.
The wind beneath the leader's wings
gives strength to those who follow

and when she tires, another leads,
so she can lead tomorrow.

If we, alone, as eagles
choose to spend our days
we'll soar, perhaps majestically
then tired, may lose our way.
As women and as leaders
our strength at times may fail
but with a team beside us
we surely will prevail.

Jeri Bawden (SI Port Angeles, Washington, USA)

Chris Knight *lives at Deception Bay, Queensland, Australia. She has been married to Graeme for 19 years. She enjoys travelling, fishing, reading and playing Lawn bowls. Professionally, Chris works for the Queensland State Government as a Senior Advisor and Internal Auditor. She is an avid SI Chatliner and has been a member of Soroptimist International for 23 years. Her passion for social justice, empowering women, and participating in community development activities has enabled her to facilitate workshops at Federation Conferences and International Conventions. Chris has held a variety of offices at Club, Region, Federation and International levels. She is currently SISWP Federation Liaison Officer for Project Sierra. Chris has recently transferred her membership to SI Pine Rivers after the dissolution of the Brisbane City Club. Chris is also a writer and has contributed articles to Soroptimist magazines, and local community radio/ media on topics relating to human rights – including violence against women and human trafficking. In 2008, Chris received the Australia Day Award for Citizen of the Year in recognition of her Soroptimist contributions to the local and global community, Chris regards herself as an earnest 'little Hobbit' who tries to make a difference where she can!*

Kindred Spirits

When I stand beside you…I feel safe and protected

When I see you smile…it warms my heart

When I look into your eyes…they sparkle like a diamond

When I hear you laugh…it lifts my spirit

When I feel uncertain…your words comfort me

When I touch your hand…I feel connected

When you are happy…I feel your joy

When I see you cry…I feel your pain and cry too

When we exchange hugs…I feel loved

When I am not with you…I sing your memory to me

When you read this…you will know how much you mean to
me

I feel blessed to call you My Soroptimist Sister, My Kindred
Spirit

Chris Knight (SI Pine Rivers Inc., Australia)

Annamarie Megrdichian *is a native Californian, born in Los Angeles, USA, the eldest of six children. She resides today in Riverside, approximately 60 miles east of L.A. She is married and has two children. She enjoys spending time entertaining friends and family at home. Annamarie has been in the financial industry most of her adult life, attempting to start her career as a teacher and changing to business when her son was young. She is currently the co-owner and Chief Financial Officer of 'AG Organics' (a soil amendment/ resource recovery company). She also holds a California Real Estate License as well as a certificate in Grantmanship. Annamarie has been a Soroptimist since 1996, joining SI Corona, before transferring to her current club, Soroptimist International of the Chino Valley. She has been Club President, as well as being a Director for three years. She is currently the District 1 Director for the Golden West Region, having been re-elected to a second term for the 2008-2010 biennium. Annamarie is considered to be both a full-time worker and a full-time volunteer, sitting on various boards throughout Riverside and San Bernadino Counties, proving that the more you give back, the better you feel!*

My Life

Life is too short
many people say;
but too often they wait
until time passes away.
Too late to make a difference
in the lives of ones we love;
We weep and we ponder
and ask God above,
"Why did I wait so long to take part,
and not share my life with the ones in my heart?"
Time is of the essence
so please don't delay;
Take time now to tell them
don't waste another day.
We *can* make a difference in the ones
that we love;
The action is up to us,
not in the good Lord above.
So stop right now and pick up the phone;
send an e-mail or letter to those folks back at home,
Letting them know that today though we're apart;
They are never that far from the love in our heart.
Take charge of our lives and those that we love;
So at night when we sleep, we thank God above,
for this life that we have and the good that it brings
and when it's our time, the angels will sing.

Annamarie Megrdichian (SI Chino Valley, California, USA)

Friends

Where would we be in this mad life without a single friend?
In good times and in bad times, when we think our world may
end!
They're always close at hand – whether living nearby or far;
Just a text, a call or an email brings them straight to where we
are.

And what about the many joys that we all share together;
Coffee, tea or lunchtime trysts, however bad the weather!
Shopping trips, weeks away, spa days or the gym;
Great fun times for sharing with the odd sad day thrown in.

Sharing tales of childhood, of our schooldays; starting work;
Dressed up for our nights out – swapping make-up as a perk!
We may find lifelong partners – or lose them along the way –
But friends will always be there – just like it was yesterday.

So imagine life without them, if you can for just a minute.
Your highs and lows, and inbetweens, with no-one sharing in
it –
No giggling in a corner; no eating forbidden food;
No putting up with frowns and sighs when you are in a mood.

And worst of all the knowledge that, when something's going
well,
There's no-one you can text or call, there's no friend you can
tell!
Life would be oh so empty if our friends just didn't exist –
So let's all treasure those we have – for they'd be sorely missed.

Linda Beddows (SI The Fylde, England)

WORK – FAMILY - LIFE

Penny Luker *was born in Pinner, Middlesex, England and now lives in Cheshire. She has worked as a teacher and head teacher and now lectures for the Open University. Her interests are her family, writing and art. Penny has been a member of Nantwich and District Soroptimists for four years and has been the press and web officer for most of that time. Her poem ' Looking Forward' is about her life and was written specifically with this book in mind. The poem 'Work' was written for National Poetry day 2008, which was on the theme of work. Penny thinks that poetry is a wonderful way of communicating.*

Work

The privilege of work
gives dignity to me.
It helps to pay my bills;
forms my identity.

Work gives me a reason
to rise and face the day
and meet lots of people;
hear what they have to say.

A variety of skills
are learned through my training.
The job gives challenges
which are brain sustaining.

Although there are some days
with tasks I could avoid,
support from my colleagues

make my days enjoyed.
There have been occasions
when I've been out of work
so now I love my job.
Contentment is my perk!

Penny Luker (SI Nantwich and District, England)

Carol Salter *lives in Manston, East Kent. England and has been a Soroptimist for 2 years. She is a member of SI Canterbury. Carol has been a nurse for 32 years and has worked in a variety of settings including being a plaster / minor operations nurse and a Charge Nurse in a drug team. In more recent years she has worked as a Health Visitor.*

Carol has also been a teacher for the last 8 years and run her own business! She loves reading, writing, cats and food – but not necessarily in that order! She has been married for 22 years and has a nine year old son. Carol's poem is about her first, but unfortunately not her last, experience being on the other side of the nursing fence. It opened her eyes to quite a few things and, she says that she hopes it has made her kinder and more tolerant as a result.

Imperfect In-patient

Every sound you hear throughout the day
Is listened to a sharper way,
For it marks the time and measures them
The hours, that you have to spend.

Endless pacing of many feet
The patients stroll, the nurses beat.
For ever nearing loud and quick

The clock of life, the tock, the tick.
Trolleys that forever rumble
Carrying drugs and tea ensemble.

You lie in bed in early morn
Enjoying moments before the dawn
Peace and comfort, semi-still
Whilst outside rain drums on the sill

The pain is strong but it's ok
As long as you're out of Sister's way.
Half past six and not up yet?
We've your bed to make, so out you get.
Not allowed back till way past one
Gee! This nursing life is fun!

Outside you hear everything that's passed
By the nurses that titter about the patient last
It's a whole new world in a strange, feared light
A traumatic way to gain insight.

A bit less sharpness, a softer tone
Would be an improvement, an essence to hone.
A little less hardness on "out you get"
Some genuine care, "yes that's great, pet"
Not thinking of money and nights – 'out there'
Leave your home life behind you with the ones that care.

Less talking so loudly for all to know
When we are weak and feeling low
Instead why not talk to us, smile with us, share;
We're not just your earnings
We're people
We're there.

Carol Salter (SI Canterbury, England)

Why Examine?

*Written for trainee examiners of LAMDA practical graded
   examinations in Communication and Performance subjects.*

It's raining and the hall is cold…
The walls are dark and bare.
Paint is peeling from them
And then, you see your chair!
Rickety legs…and a wooden seat,
A tiny table too…
The day before you yawns with dread
As you smell a 'soggy sock' stew!
The steward struggles at a very slow pace,
And candidates all come late…
Your coffee is cold, and a sandwich appears
Well past its sell-by-date!
The cold sets in around your feet
And overall standards are weak.
Voices are thin…diction is slack,
The roof is beginning to leak…
Then…with a smile, and a breath of fresh air,
A performance lights up like dawn
The words lift from print and a face comes alive,
For a second…a magic is born.
The early alarm; the rain-spotted streets…
The day now seems to fly!
You know, in that special moment,
The answer to your question,
'Why?'

Jacque Emery (SI Canterbury, England)

Ann Reeves *was born in London, but has lived all her life in Kent, England. She currently lives in a small village between Ashford and Folkestone – not far from the end of the Channel Tunnel. She is a teacher, working in a Boys' Grammar School in Ashford, teaching Technology. This is mainly graphics, but there is some work with the younger boys using wood, metal and plastics. Ann has 2 children. She claims to have been a Soroptimist since she was in her late teens, when her mother joined SI Ashford and she helped her at a number of events. She sold raffle tickets, served coffee, took money at the door for special events – and is sure that, for a long time, it was not noticed that she was not officially a member! She did finally join in 1992 and since then was Club President in 2000-2001 and Regional President for South East England in 2006-2007. She is currently Regional Secretary. As a teacher of technology, it comes as no surprise that Ann enjoys making things – including noticeboards, photo greetings cards, engraved glassware for special occasions and, most recently, beaded necklaces.*

A (Birth)day in the life of…

"Happy birthday Mum,
Just stay in bed,
Here, open your cards!"
My daughter said.

"Happy birthday Mum,
Just stay in bed,
I'll bring you breakfast!"
My young son said.

"Happy birthday Dear,
Just stay in bed,
We've got a problem!"
My husband said.

The washing machine broke
So the floor is wet,
The carpets ruined
No end to it yet
The paint is flaking
The floor tiles are up
The underlay squelches
Overflowing's my cup.

"Happy birthday Mum,
Just stay in bed,
Happy birthday indeed!"
I said.

Ann Reeves (SI Ashford, England)

Mary Cossaboon *was raised in a large family in northern New Jersey, USA. She is a public school music teacher in southern New Jersey and has taught band and orchestral instruments for over 30 years. She is married and has two daughters. For an end of senior high school project, parents were asked to write 'advice' to their college-bound children, and she wrote the following poem for her youngest daughter. Since the class had been studying old English works, Mary had some fun composing her words of 'Motherly Advice'. Mary has been a member of Soroptimist International of Cumberland County since 2006.*

Motherly Advice to Claire

My dearest, youngest daughter yet,
As you prepare to set your fate,
To travel off a college set,
How my heart will burst that date.

How quickly seems this time did go,
From whence the sweetest babe be known
Whose head abound with curly locks
A woman, full and tall has grown,
So beautiful, poised, kind and knowledge known,
My heart doth burst with pride.
There are now things I must repeat
So stay now there upon thy seat,
Take heed to what I write now here,
Thou has't heard it all throughout the years.

When thou art out and 'on your own'
Remember all the warnings said,
To bolt thy door and tuck thy cash,
Call home at night before thy bed.

Take heed against thy counterparts,
That is for males can break thy heart
If choice be made, I warn to thee,
To turn that game away from thee.

Spend thy money wisely now,
For everything made to see, doth cost,
To pay for things we know not how,
when on frivolous trinkets dollars lost.

In math, and language, history,
And study Art in classes must,
Spend thy bulk of time not free,
But with pen and ink and paint do lust.

For thy talent, has not yet been seen,
Bloomed in one so new and young,
To see a face and draw it down,
As if that face 'looked' back at thee.

Remember all you have been taught,
Important is and what is not,
New friends dependable, may be
But for comfort stays touched old.

Remember thy Maker and His Son,
Who loved thee first before any one,
Whose Peace and Love will leave thee light,
Seek Him first for all that's Right.

Remember all we, who in our hearts,
Hold thee so dear and true,
There is not a time of day or night,
We will not think of you,
And love you for eternity no matter come what may,
Dearest daughter, sister, friend,
As we love thee today,
Our hearts doth burst with pride.

Mary Cossaboon (SI Cumberland County, New Jersey, USA)

***Sally Shears** was born in Bradford, Yorkshire, England. Her career was spent mainly working with a range of disadvantaged young people. Latterly she was Area Director for West Yorkshire for a National Charity. Sally has two sons, two grandchildren and three step-grandchildren. Her family moved to the Lake District when her sons were small and they grew up in idyllic countryside taking part in a range of outdoor activities. She was widowed at the age of 50 and has now re-married and moved to the Crook of Lune, which is a lovely river valley on*

the border of Lancashire and Yorkshire. Sally is a Justice of the
Peace in Preston and is very busy with court sittings, committees
and training. She is a keen walker and outdoor enthusiast and
walks every day, watching the kingfishers and otters who live
by the river. She is a member of the University of the Third Age
and is currently taking part in Geology, Yoga and Calligraphy.
She is also interested in cricket. Sally first joined Soroptimist
International when she moved to Lancashire and made many
friends through the organisation. She has been Vice President
and President of the Garstang Club. Poetry is her great
relaxation. Sally loves reading and writing it and is only truly
relaxed when she has a pen in her hand and ideas in her head.

The Soroptimist at Sixty

We were sixty last month
My husband Fred and me
It's funny how that number
Can have such piquancy
When I was sixteen last year
I never thought I'd reach
This great and worldly wisdom
That gives me power to teach
The young in all their glory
To live life to the full
Alas, they all know better
And think my advice dull

But me and Fred, we reckon
We've hit upon the truth
We'll share it with you if you like
To laugh at misspent youth
Fred wants to be eccentric
A pony tail he'll wear
Dig out his sixties trousers

You know, the ones with flare
See Stonehenge at Midsummer
And get a motorbike
Get down at hip rock concerts
Do all the things we like

No more spick and span-ness
And keeping things for best
We'll wear the latest fashions
But always with a vest
The kids all think we're crackers
They say we've lost the plot
They're worried that our health won't last
The temperature's much too hot
Our answer is "We've earned it",
And Fred says, "Do we care
We're doing what we want to
Now we've got time to spare?"

For we're the original Rockers
We just went quiet for a while
To raise you and make sure you
Could start your lives with style
But now we've lost our shackles
Again we're wild and free
With just a hint of aching joints
But that won't worry me
We're off to spend the winters
Somewhere exotic and hot
Share in the local colour
Maybe smoke some you know what

So children and grandchildren
Prepare to see us less
And start to stand on your own feet
And sort out your own mess
For we'll be out of 'phone range

Doing tango, salsa, twist
Trying all the local drinks
Your inheritance at risk
Ignoring creaking muscles
In our own new rave
Get used to living your own lives
As we start to SPEND NOT SAVE.

Sally Shears (SI Garstang, England)

Linda Glaser *was born and raised on a family owned (4th generation) Hereford Cattle and Quarter Horse Ranch in Northeastern Nevada (Elko) USA. She is the eldest of two children. Linda gained a Bachelor of Science Degree in Animal Science and a Master's Degree in Education from the University of Nevada. She spent 8 years as a Buyer/Assistant Manager of a Western Store. This was followed by 15 years as a Youth and Livestock Specialist for the University of Nevada Cooperative Extension Service, which involved leadership training and curriculum development for programs such as the National 4-H Aerospace Project. For the last 20 years Linda has owned a travel agency and worked as a tour conductor. She is currently living in Northern California as a full time caregiver for aging parents Linda joined Soroptimist International of Yerington, Nevada, in 1992. She served as President for 2 years, developed the Sierra Nevada Region E-blast Communications system and served as Communications Coordinator for 4 years. Linda is currently Region Roster Coordinator. She does not have a Soroptimister of her own at present, but has been inspired by the time volunteered and generosity of her local 'significant others' in a small rural community!*

Salute to Soroptimisters

A big salute to Soroptimisters in our local communities
    everywhere.
We are strong independent women, but when we need
    assistance you are there.
Be it toting, tugging, hauling, lifting, building or even flipping
    pancakes
You are but a phone call away ready to do whatever it takes.

Many times our Soroptimist volunteer projects are involved
    and extensive,
But we can count on your generous contributions when it gets
    too expensive.
It may be volunteering for fund raisers or just opening your
    wallet…
Your time is precious and we are grateful for your effort…
    whatever you call it.

To others you may be just another face in the large crowd
But when my star is shining I know you are there standing
    proud.
And whether our Soroptimist successes are local or in
    countries abroad
You are always at the head of the line ready to congratulate and
    applaud.

Not just anyone can be a Soroptimister, the title must be
    earned…
The required qualities come from within and seldom can be
    learned.
A big heart, compassion for others and a positive considerate
    attitude
Make you a Soroptimister who is worthy of our deepest
    gratitude!

Linda Glaser (SI Yerington, Nevada, USA)

Looking Forward

The sands of time once trickled,
are now pouring at a pace;
but my life is full of treasures
as part of the human race.

My husband's wise and gentle
and my children, they are kind.
Now their children are arriving,
who knows what world they'll find!

My teaching time is over
but I'll remember all my days,
the buzz that came when children
were performing Christmas plays.

The pupils were so honest
and very keen to learn.
I seldom found them trouble
or needed to be stern.

Nowadays my life is filled
with friends and optimism
and I enjoy the many projects
which are 'Soroptimism'.

Penny Luker (SI Nantwich and District, England)

The Diet

I've just stood on the scales
What a dreadful fright.
I really thought my jeans had shrunk again!
What I didn't realise
Was, they're getting far too tight,
No chips and crisps and cakes for me – that's plain.
I'll try to lose a stone –
That's well within my reach,
Before the summer comes and clothes get less!
Bikini's don't look good
If you're bulging on the beach –
And I doubt if I can do up my best dress!
So that's my new idea –
Nothing will change my mind,
Not anything you do or eat or say!
Some chocolates – just for me.
Oh thank you – that's so kind.
A diet? Well- perhaps another day!

Jacque Emery (SI Canterbury, England)

Erene Grieve *lives in Milford Haven, Pembrokeshire, Wales. She left school at 15 and went to University when she was 37. She started teaching when she was 40 and acquired her own bike for the first time at the age of 45! Now retired from teaching she operates the 'Stamps in Schools Project', introducing children to the joys of stamp collecting. Erene has been a member of SI Milford Haven for 12 years. In her spare time she enjoys cycling the Welsh cycle-ways with her husband, Alan, and writing the occasional article, short story or poem.*

The Bike Ride (1955)

I borrowed a bike from my friend's Dad
And followed my friend down Primrose Lane
I wobbled and quaked the tow path route
On cobbles and kerbs I wove my way
I hollered and laughed to show my joy
I wallowed in freedom, and down the hill
I offered to race my friend back home
I bobbled and hovered and finally fell
I hobbled back home to see my Mum
She cuddled me well and fed me jam
She covered my wounds and dried my tears
I gobbled my tea of chips and ham.
But this isn't the truth, in fact it's lies,
The Dad of my friend had no such ties,
And Primrose Lane was a dark back alley,
The tow path route had a sign 'No Entry'.
My laughter and joy were far from the truth;
I hated my bike ride and my friend Ruth.
And mother was out (as she always was),
I tended myself and got on with my jobs.
And even the memory of chips and ham
Was far from true – it was probably Spam.
And now that I'm sixty and riding a Marin
I wobble and bobble with my man Alan
And on occasions I hover and fall
But I pick myself up and don't cry at all.

Erene Grieve (SI Milford Haven, Wales)

Peggy Gentile-Van Meter *lives in Cumberland County, New Jersey, USA. She has a Bachelors Degree in Social Studies and a Masters degree in Holocaust and Genocide Studies. Peggy is currently working as a teacher of Social Studies, United States History and Western Civilization. She is a member of numerous professional bodies, including Cumberland County College Leadership, for which she is an Advisory Board Member and a Team Project Advisor. She was Vice President of Cumberland Regional Education Association from 2007-2008. She has also been very involved with staff development leadership activities at the College of New Jersey, training tomorrow's teachers, and with a variety of student development programs. Peggy has received a number of awards and recognition for her service to education and was Cumberland Regional Teacher of the Year in 2006. Peggy is committed to working for her community. She is a member of both Lions and Soroptimist International and is currently the Co-Chair for SI Cumberland County's project, the Matri-Ark Center – helping women become productive members of their communities. Peggy is a Board member of 'The Alliance Against Substance Abuse' and 'Cumberland County Coalition for Holocaust and Genocide Education'. Peggy also serves her community in a different way, by being a hostess for the Miss Cumberland County Scholarship Pageant.*

Chapters in a Book

My, a half-century here, and I begin to wonder what legacy I
    will leave.
The years have gone by, and I wonder where they went.
Who have I met? Who have I loved?
Who has loved me?
Daughter, Mother, Wife, Teacher, Friend...A Woman.
The events turn like pages in a book...
Some great chapters, some slow chapters, some sad chapters,
    and many happy chapters...

How will the book end? It will not be a best seller, but the
    compassion and love that can be found in the pages will
    perhaps help someone find their way.
My life is like a book, and the best part, I can write and rewrite
the future chapters.
I can be sure that I have been the best at what I love the most.
When I have stumbled, when I have fallen, I have only had to
    glance up
and have had the warmth of family or friends reach out to me.
My life, as simple as it might seem to some, has been filled
    with rewards, for I have learned the importance of love,
    friendship, respect and responsibility.
I know that one step at a time, and one smile at a time,
I have reached and touched the lives of many.
The numerous faces that have touched my life will remain
    etched in
my heart and mind forever.

Peggy Gentile-Van Meter (SI Cumberland County, New Jersey,
USA)

Sandra Donald *was born of Jamaican parents in Dulwich,*
South London, England. She is married and lives in
Kensington,Central London. She works as a Property Developer
with concerns in London and South Africa. Sandra is also a keen
singer. She is continuing to build on her experience as a musician
and as such is currently studying a Vocal Diploma Course at
Vocaltech in London. She has been a member of Soroptimist
International of Greater London for five years. In 2007 she
performed in a fundraising concert of Gospel, Soul and Jazz at
'Pizza on the Park' in Knightsbridge, London, organized by her
club and raising money for Project Independence. She is currently
her Club President.

My Life Hope

Hope is a drug, and has the strong hold on my heart
It's with me first thing in the morning, and as I lay my head to
    rest at night
Like coffee it's that adrenalin rush when everything around me
    seems to be falling apart!
Reaching out through the darkness and despair I find hope
    unshaken but not stirred shining so bright!

Hope moves within me with every intake of breath
Its inspiration brings a knowing that better things are to come,
    and
With its open hand it gives me the courage to close the door on
    all negative thoughts
And as I glance over my shoulder I see hope waiting, and I
    calmly walk toward its burning light of hope

Hope provides me with the positive mindset to afford
    continued good health
It gives me the strength to keeping showing love, allowing
    myself to be loved and to support and, to care for those I
    love the most
It fills me with a strength and boldness, which drives me to
    continue on life's paths with a focused determination but
    always with my friend HOPE

So let's have three cheers for HOPE.

Sandra Donald (SI Greater London, England)

50:50/5
a reaction to a diagnosis of cancer and the harsh treatment of chemotherapy

Errant mitotic messages
bring no stalking sepulchral shade,
unleashing, rather, floods of light,
clear focus, celebration,
and gales of comic opportunity.
Dissected nerves signal arm and shoulder
flayed to the bone,
this palpable calumny easily discounted
for joyful reality –
the scalpel skimming off the crust of custom
from the world:
from the exaltation of lark-rinsed mornings
to nightingale-throbbing dark,
the wide wold-walk of wind
to vein-traced petal or wing,
brimming with blessing,
each instar of colour, note and flavour
ecdysed till new-made,
the beloved a heart-burst
of that first love free fall,
of cradling a new-born son,
when time / heart / beat
stops
still;
the uncertain future but a new
adventure.

Clare Harding (SI Blackburn, England)

From one who swears not by the moon

Pharmaceutical mercenaries crawl
      under the skin,
Detonating neural grenades,
      answering sniper fire,
Perpetrating poison in bloated
      ice-laden pools;
The heart
      lurches
  reels
          recoils
  blindly punch-drunk;
Sentries strain to glimpse, through months of hooded night-
  watches,
mithril star-glimmer;
Beaten to its knees in blood
      the bruised body
      still
      will
      not confess or yield,
In the face of its tormentors
      throws love.

Clare Harding (SI Blackburn, England)

Progression

Across the bay I see a moulded hill
comfortable with its pregnant shape
timeless, waiting

in Ruakaka Bay, a storm rages around us
we wait, secure, the fire hums
and the water tanks are full

the woman I see in the hill waits too
she will give birth
and pick up the pieces of her life

never to be the same

Frances Meech (SI Wellington, New Zealand)

Gungor Aribal *was born in Manisa, Turkey. After graduating from Mersin High School, she entered the academy of Fine Arts in Istanbul, specialising in ceramics. Between 1980-1991, she was the President of the Painters' Society. In 1982, she got a license degree from the Academy of Fine Arts in Traditional Turkish Handicrafts and in 1984, was awarded Honorary Membership by the Italian Arts and Culture Association. She became one of the founder members of Mersin High School Graduates Society in 1985. Gungor is currently President of the Recreation Society – a role she has held since 1992. She is also a member of both the Turkish Tourism and the Mediterranean States Writers and Journalists Societies.She has received an honorary Doctorate from the World Academy of Arts and Culture – of which she is a member. In addition, she was honoured as an Ambassador of Humanitarianism in 2006, by the USA Ambassadors' Society. Gungor's works are found in museums and private collections both in Turkey and all over the world. They include ceramic walls, wall reliefs and panels. Her most recent works include a large ceramic monumental wall in Adana's Province House and a hanging monumental wall in Edirne. She was named as the 'Outstanding Professional Artist' from ABI (USA) in 2001, in the fields of ceramics, painting and poetry. She has been working as Art Director of the 'Ankara Art Magazine', 'Mother' magazine and 'Young Generation' newspaper. She has also published three books of poetry. Gungor is a member of Soroptimist International of Sisli, Istanbul. Poetry and art are a way of living for her, and she dedicates herself to social relations and the welfare of humanity.*

I want to Survive

I want to survive
Even though life leaves the body
I want to survive
In the sound of the winds
In the white of the clouds
In the green of the grass
I want to smell
Like spring
In the dreams of my beloved
I want to expand my life
Even if I die
Beloved
In the waves of the seas
In the sand of the deserts
In the place beyond your eyes
In the middle of your dreams
I want to be of your faith
Fertility of your existence
Reality of death
I want to be born again
To laugh and cry with you
To live the same dream
Over and over with you
I want to catch the space
I want to be a light, a sound
I want to be a breath in you
A breath
I want to be a breath

Güngör D Arıbal (SI Sisli, Turkey)

VAR OLMAK İSTİYORUM

Var olmak istiyorum
Can bedeni terk etse de
Rüzgârların sesinde
Bulutların beyazında
Çimenin yeşilinde
Buram buram
Bahar kokmak istiyorum
Sevgilinin düşlerinde
Yaşamak İstiyorum
Sürdürmek varlığımı
Ölsem de!…
Sevdalım
Denizlerin dalgasında
Çöllerin kumunda
Ve gözlerinin ardında
Hayallerinin tam ortasında
Kaderinin rahmeti,
Varlığının bereketi,
Ölümün gerçeği olmak istiyorum.
Yeniden doğmak istiyorum
Seninle gülmek, ağlamak
Bir rüyayı tekrar tekrar
Seninle yaşamak istiyorum
Kainatı yakalamak.
Sende bir ışık, bir ses
Bir nefes olmak istiyorum.
Bir nefes
Bir nefes olmak istiyorum.

Güngör D Arıbal (SI Sisli, Turkey)

OUR SOROPTIMISM

Pat Fergusson *was brought up in Skipton, Yorkshire, England. She learnt to read by recognising the rhyming couplets of Rupert Bear in the Daily Express, which possibly started her fascination with words and poetry.Pat loves word-play and the wry humour of Yorkshire. As an art teacher,she taught ceramics, changing direction to management training and latterly working as an English lecturer. She has lived in Lancashire for most of her working life.Her love of language continues as she now works as a proof-reader. She does not find this to be a popular role as she feels that punctuation and grammar are neither sexy nor greatly used! Joining SI Chorley a dozen years ago, Pat had the dubious distinction of closing the club as President after a successful 61st year. She transferred to The Fylde and is looking forward to being President in the coming year. Pat's home life involves a motley group of adult children and grandchildren, all far-flung. She loves being out of doors, gardening, walking and enjoying the tremendous variety in England's climate and countryside.*

Poem

Soroptimists, it's said, just do it all,
Us ladies – old, young, large and small,
Keen to support – who, what, why, when,
We've got it all – except for men.

Pat Fergusson (SI The Fylde, formerly SI Chorley, England)

June Gabbitas *was born in Barnsley, South Yorkshire, England and her working background was as a nurse and midwife. She served for 8 years as an officer in Queen Alexandra's Royal Army Nursing Corps. This took her to Germany, Hong Kong, Nepal, Catterick and Berlin. Her career in The National Health Service culminated in being Chief Nurse of an NHS Trust hospital in South Yorkshire. June now works as a volunteer bereavement worker for Cruse Bereavement Care Cumbria and is an active member of the newly formed First Responder group in Grange over Sands where she now lives. In the past, June travelled to Romania working in a maternity hospital and orphanages for a period of some ten years, as a volunteer. Her first visit was only six months after the revolution in that country. June is married with two stepchildren and four grandchildren. Her Soroptimist career started in 1998 and she has been club President and Regional President for North West England and the Isle of Man 2006-2007. She is currently the Project Sierra Ambassador for the Region. She says that she is lucky to belong to a very proactive club with some wonderful members. According to June, her poem is very 'tongue in cheek', and the first that she has ever written!*

Oh! To be a Poet Laureate
with apologies to Pam Ayres!

I've never written a poem before,
where on earth do you begin?
I've never thought that I could before,
but I've finally got stuck in.

I've never written a poem before,
and this one has a real theme.
Soroptimists are whom it's about,
their work, their hopes, their dreams.

I know they have lots of meetings
and they're always flying the flag,

But what's all this friendship and eating
and what's in their bright blue bags?

They talk about Programme Focus,
Community, peace and war.
They're always up to some raucous,
doing this, doing that, doing more.

They certainly have lots of influence.
The UN, they say, has to listen.
They're known for their primness and prudence
and their grey hair and zeal for a mission.

If you are down and out and
    You haven't much clout
these women are the women for you.
They'll badger and chatter
    with those who most matter
and sort out your problems right through.

I've never written a poem before
and most probably won't again.
But I've tried and I'm keen
and I've stuck to the theme
So that's it, had a go, that's the end.

June Gabbitas (SI Grange over Sands, England)

Soropti – What?

Soroptimists – oh what a mixture
They're dynamic or whacky and fun
Sometimes they're all three in one bundle
Depending whose company they're in

Dynamic when talking with passion
About something that's close to their heart
Like nappies, or AIDS and street children,
Contact centres, beach clean – where to start?

Whacky – with fundraising hats on
Be it homeless or limbless to aid –
Sleeping outside a store raising money?
Now that's 'over and above' I'm afraid!

Fun when it comes to explaining
What Soroptimists are – what they pursue
For it's all about friendship and teamwork
And making things worthwhile to do

With Soroptimists you never go hungry
Or thirsty – and breakfasts are good
Oh and don't forget birthdays and charters
And other excuses for food!

So next time you are asked what your badge is
Just say it's an image that reflects
Many fun times helping very good causes
With the dozens of friends that you've met!

Linda Beddows (SI The Fylde, England)

Anne Quainoo *was born on the Isle of Anglesey, Wales. She is
fluent in the Welsh language and was not taught English formally
until she was 7 years old. She trained as a teacher in Liverpool,
England and Bangor, North Wales. Anne taught in Anglesey for
9 years before moving to Heysham, Lancashire, where she was
Head of the Economics and Business Studies Department at
Heysham High School for 22 years. She retired from teaching in
1995 and currently lives in Lancaster. Anne is still very involved
with GCSE examination work in Business and Communication
Systems. Her hobbies are holidaying, reading, knitting, sudoku
and crosswords. Anne is married to James, who originates from
Ghana, West Africa, and they have 2 children and one grand-
child. She has a sister who lives in Cairo, Egypt – which Anne
says is good for holidays! Anne has been a Soroptimist since
1989. She was initially a member of SI Morecombe and Heysham
and was President 1994/5 but transferred to SI Lancaster on her
retirement. She became President 1998/9, Regional Treasurer
1999/2003, Regional President 2003/4 and currently holds the
post of Regional Extension and Membership Officer. Anne was
encouraged to write poems by Elizabeth Woolf, a gifted artist and
former Soroptimist.*

Best of Sisters

*The 'Red Rose' refers to Past President of Soroptimist
    International, Lynn Dunning.*

We are a line of sisterhood with ribbons gold and blue
Stretching downward through the years since 1942.
It couldn't have been easy in that far off time,
With hardship, war and shortages and military clime.
Truly 'Best of Sisters', as our emblem reads
Friendship can speak volumes with smiles and worthy deeds.

But here we are together, all of one accord,
With lots of things to celebrate and many to applaud.

We welcome all new members with friendship and warm
    greeting,
With very splendid shortbread and coffee every meeting.
Truly 'Best of Sisters', as our emblem reads
Friendship can speak volumes with smiles and worthy deeds.

We have friendship links with Denmark, Anglesey in Wales
And Lancaster, Pennsylvania where a special link prevails.
From them our Candle Ceremony which brings both smile and
    tear
A moving evening is enjoyed with friendship and good cheer.
Truly 'Best of Sisters', as our emblem reads
Friendship can speak volumes with smiles and worthy deeds.

The Senior Coffee Morning is something to behold,
And Mother Christmas visits with her generous sack of gold.
Barbecues and Safaris are always being planned,
With every member ready to lend a helping hand.
Truly 'Best of Sisters', as our emblem reads
Friendship can speak volumes with smiles and worthy deeds.

The Programme Action Ladies meet on Saturdays for hours on
    ends
And talk and plan and plan and talk but always part good
    friends;
Because they have enjoyed a feast – a lunch second to none,
But only partake of the food – when all the work is done!
Truly 'Best of Sisters', as our emblem reads
Friendship can speak volumes with smiles and worthy deeds.

There are many things we do to contribute to life.
To make it just enjoyable and not a time of strife.
For international efforts many goals we've scored,
With stamps and coins and knitting, helping life abroad.
Truly 'Best of Sisters', as our emblem reads
Friendship can speak volumes with smiles and worthy deeds.

The service we give locally is varied and sincere
And many people benefit – this is obviously very clear.
It hasn't been so easy to cover all the things
That make our Club so special as we tackle what life brings.
Truly 'Best of Sisters', as our emblem reads
Friendship can speak volumes with smiles and worthy deeds.

Our own Red Rose from Ramsbottom will soon realise her
    dream
When she's installed in Denver, what will be her theme?
'Imagine', this Lancashire Lady with her 'International' flag
    unfurled,
Bringing understanding and goodwill all around the world.
Truly 'Best Of Sisters', as our emblem reads
Friendship can speak volumes with smiles and worthy deeds.

Lancaster Soroptimists may we go forward, good and true,
Continuing all that has been achieved since 1942.
We salute our Red Rose City, dignified and serene
And God Bless the Duke of Lancaster, Her Majesty the Queen.
Truly 'Best of Sisters', as our emblem reads
Friendship can speak volumes with smiles and worthy deeds.

Anne Quainoo (SI Lancaster, England)

Carolyn Lowe *has lived in Carnforth, Lancashire, England since
1986. She worked for Lancashire Fire and Rescue Service for 35
years and was awarded the Queen's Medal for Long Service and
Good Conduct. She retired from her position as Area Admin
Manager in 2006. Carolyn has been a Soroptimist since 1993.
She was President 1999-2000 when her charity was Guide Dogs
for the Blind which led her on to become Secretary to the local
branch of the Association. She is sharing the role of President
both this year and next, when her club celebrates its Silver
Jubilee.*

The International Soroptimist

Who has aims and objectives on which she builds her life?
Who can be a mother, friend, sister, aunt or wife?
Who believes in human rights to build a better world for all?
Who will fight against prejudice to overcome the highest wall?
Who's always there when you need a helping hand?
Who has high ethical standards and strives to understand?
Who arrives for meetings despite cold and wind and rain?
Whose goal is service, time and time again?
Who has a busy lifestyle, balancing family, work and pleasure?
Who has so many talents it's impossible to measure?
Who leaps into programme action the minute she is tasked?
Who comes up with an answer as soon as she is asked?
Who has a worldwide invitation to find friendship old and
    new?
Who has an emblem of raised arms and coloured in gold and
    blue?
Who can entertain you with a feast befitting for a Queen?
Who will dress up in fancy outfits, the like of which you've
    never seen?
Who can be serious when problems are running deep?
Who can make you laugh out loud or comfort whilst you
    weep?
Who would never mention she's done anything worthy of a
    shout?
Any International Soroptimist, because that's what it's about.

Carolyn Lowe (SI Carnforth, England)

Jill Lazard *is a retired Medical Practitioner. She qualified
in 1957 at The University of Cape Town (UCT) and lived in
Salisbury (Harare) for 18 months as a government Medical
Officer. She then returned to Cape Town where she worked at
Groote Schuur Hospital for 45 years. Jill was in a variety of
departments – her last being a Family Planning and Menopause
clinic, where she stayed for 26 years. She also ran a private
Obesity clinic for many years. Jill retired three years ago. Jill was
a doctors' daughter, became a doctor and married a doctor! She
has 4 children – 3 sons and a daughter and 7½ grandchildren.
Jill has been a Soroptimist since 1987 and was National President
and Federation Officer from 1998-2002. She also has many other
interests including being a Founder and Chairperson on the Fine
and Decorative Arts Society in Cape Town and being a member
of the Hospital Board of New Somerset Hospital and organiser
of their 150 year celebrations. Jill is also involved in the Gardens
Synagogue, working as a guide and organising a Sound and
Light show,as it is the oldest Congregation in South Africa. She
has represented Western Cape in table-tennis and only gave up
competitive tennis 3 years ago.*

A Toast To Soroptimists On International Day

A toast to Soroptimists is on board
The best of sisters we are called
Every year on December ten
International night is celebrated again

A Federation of Four
Unites us even more
For wherever in the world you roam
Soroptimists will have a home

They are sisters who work for love and good
And the upliftment of Womanhood

The principles are very clear
Though not many know that we are here
To work for higher ethics in life
And for human rights without strife
To develop the spirit of being a friend
And to promote service without end
For part of the United Nations are we
Where we help to keep the world free
Thus around the world we candles light
To keep Soroptimism shining bright
Please raise your glass and drink a toast
To Soroptimists – your Honoured Host.

Jill Lazard (SI Cape of Good Hope, South Africa)

Chain of Office

*Lines written on handing over the President's Chain when
   President SI Bootle 2003/4*

Links to the past
in Presidents' names,
Memories live of
grand old dames;
Hats and gloves
and an order, rare...
Formidable, strong;
They dared to care.
Changing lives
and customs too,
Remember the old
but welcome the new;
Challenging women
for sixty-two years,
To think of their sisters,
alleviate fears.
Fun and friendship

from age to age,
Handed on
as we turn the page
To another world
and a future bold,
In the chain of an office
yet to be told.

Jacque Emery (SI Canterbury, England)

The New Style Soroptimist!

Kindness, caring and thoughtfulness too
Patience and listening skills, and people who
Look after others and tend to their needs
And think of the future and plant a few seeds
In the minds of the public to make sure they know
To raise their awareness and ensure they grow
To care about poverty in war ridden zones
To look after children without any homes
Research all problems, make people discover
That they can do something to help one another.
A difficult task but one that is done
Each day, everywhere, both abroad and at home.

So feel very proud to be part of the team
Sorops are the best – you could say they're the cream!
From all walks of life – with professional background
They carry out duties – but without ever a sound
Hardly anyone knows who they are or where from:
But Soroptimists are changing – they are banging their drum.
So prepare for the new style – with PR and flair
They'll be along shortly – and let anyone dare
To try and go back to the quiet old ways!
They are gone now forever – in Time's misty haze!

But – the aims and the objects will always remain
The caring, the friendship, the easing of pain
So a new style Soroptimist I shall be as a member
And let's hope that we flourish and grow in our number
For without us the world will be poorer no doubt
So let's all spread the word and give SI some clout!!
Emphasise all the fun and the friendships you've gained
And explain why a member all these years you've remained
Perhaps if we all try together we'll find
New members just like us – caring and kind!

Linda Beddows (SI The Fylde, England)

Hilary Allinson *was born in the North East of England.*
Interested in fashion, she began her career as a buyer for
Binns in Sunderland and opened her own fashion boutique in
Lancaster. She finally became Manager for Lakeland Fashion in
Ambleside, before taking retirement. As a Soroptimist, Hilary
was a founder member of SI Carnforth and has held the offices of
Social Secretary, Treasurer and President. She is currently Joint
President. Hilary has made many friends in Soroptimism and
attended several conferences. She is interested in art, photography
and gardening, walking and entertaining. She is married to Ted.
They do not have any children but their two dogs, Herbie – a Jack
Russell Terrier, and Albert, a Springer Spaniel, keep them busy.

The Business Meeting

A Wednesday night and the time is near
To leave my husband and disappear
I'm rushing off to the local inn
I can assure you it's not to drink gin!

Tonight is Carnforth's business meeting
Just time to give old friends a greeting
Aims and objectives are proudly read
The agenda for the evening before us spread.

The treasurer's report does seem healthy
As a small club we're not very wealthy
"Do subs have to go up?" we groan
"Yes" say the powers that be – we moan.

Programme Action is what it's about
Whatever the problem we'll sort it out
Women and children – whatever the call
We're there to help – human rights for all.

We abhor the atrocities of war
We rush round collecting money 'till our feet are sore
Soroptimists are always there to lend a helping hand
We're the very best of sisters spread across the land.

A social get together the next time we meet
Lots of good food and wine. Oh what a treat!
The decisions are all made, the meeting's at an end
Time to say goodnight to each and every friend.

Hilary Allinson (SI Carnforth, England)

Tracey Lowther *was born in Glendale (California, USA) in
1943 and grew up in the San Fernando Valley. She married
Robert and they have two children and five grandchildren. They
live in the beautiful Mojave desert region of Hesperia. Tracey
is the Campaign Director and Event co-ordinator for her local
'Desert Communities United Way' – a rewarding job which
she loves because she can help her community. Tracey became
a Soroptimist 9 years ago (SI Victor Valley) and in 2006 she
chartered the Apple Valley club which was one of her most
rewarding experiences. She has been President of both clubs
and has held almost all the elected positions – except Treasurer!
Tracey enjoys being a Soroptimist because the organization can
accomplish a lot to make the world a better place. Tracey and her
husband enjoy four-wheeling together. They also love gardening
– and with 3 acres, have plenty to do!*

World

Our Soroptimist world
Each club's portion so small
We fill it with friends
With a quest to serve all

Soroptimism our passion
Rebuilding lives is our goal
We search out the disadvantaged
Adding to our portion ten fold

Our cup full of blessings
Overflows as we pray
And our portion gets larger
As we volunteer each day

Tracey Lowther (SI Apple Valley, California, USA)

Marion Forrest *lives in Garstang, Lancashire, England and was a member of SI Preston for over 20 years. She was President twice. Marion worked as a Director of Personnel in the National Health Service before her retirement in 2001 due to ill health. She now works as a volunteer in a Police Station and also in a Sue Ryder charity shop. Marion is married to Derek. Her leisure time is mainly taken up with her computer, swimming and holidays – especially in her caravan.*

Soroptimist International

Sisters of the world together
Offering service and whatever,
Raising funds for our charities
Over here and overseas.

Pals you'll meet and fun abound,
Take the time to get around.
In our friendships we are strong,
Members new we hope will throng.

Interesting meetings we must hold
So our subjects must be bold
Topical, out there and rational
      We are
Soroptimist International.

Marion Forrest (formerly SI Preston, England)

Kris Pearson *has been a member of Soroptimist International of Wellington, New Zealand for almost twenty years. She is a Past President, Friendship Links Co-ordinator, and enjoys hosting pot-luck dinners for visiting Soroptimists. After a long career as an advertising writer, Kris now works up a ladder with her husband, as a curtain installer. She insists that this accounts for the sensible shoes and very strong shoulders. To offset the shoes and shoulders she spends her spare time as a romance writer!*

Every Third Thursday

Every third Thursday my heart's a little lighter,
My eyes a little brighter, my step has extra spring.
Favourite friends are meeting, and we shuffle round the
    seating.
We're certain Thursday's chat has extra zing.
I love these ladies dearly. We're close as sisters, really.
Once a month on Thursday eyes all gleam.
Wellington was chartered by women now departed –
the first New Zealand club to join the team.
And seventy years later the need is even greater
to work where we can do the greatest good.
We listen and we plan, carefully as we can,
Hoping we can help in sisterhood.

So what's the news from Region? And Federation, too?
Where's a worthwhile project? And how much can we do?
Soroptimists of Wellington will help where there's a need.
Once a month on Thursday, with a speaker and a feed!

Kris Pearson (SI Wellington New Zealand)

Moya Coates *wrote her poem as a result of watching and participating in the first electronic voting at the Bournemouth Conference, England in 2004. She was President of Soroptimist International of Carnforth and District at the time and therefore the voting delegate. Everyone was bemused and she wrote the poem between votes. She said that somehow, they all managed in the end! Since then Moya has been Regional rep and is now splitting her time between the UK and New Zealand where she has 3 very young grandchildren. This has enabled her to take part in meetings in the Christchurch club and she has made some wonderful friends there. Her time in the UK is spent fund raising for the National Society of the Prevention of Cruelty to Children (NSPCC) and she is currently Chair of the local committee. Moya also visits a local primary school and assesses children who are having difficulties, drawing up Individual Education Programmes for them. Living where she does, Moya can indulge her passion for fell walking. She also plays badminton in her local team.*

Ode to Electronic Voting
Inspired at the Bournemouth Conference 2004

Press the button now
Like this that's how
However we vote no-one can see
At our last meeting did we agree
On this motion, that motion, amendment three?
Up on the screen green graph and red
Check with your notes – is that what we said?
This new-fangled technology
What a to-do
Minutes via e-mail, web sites too
Soroptimism moves forwards
Do you?

Moya Coates (SI Carnforth, England)

In the Club

Why are we in the Club?
To do good works – to meet new friends
To socialize – it all depends
On who we are as to why we join.

Why are we in the Club?
To help our sisters – brothers too
To give ourselves something to do
To give back to the community!

Why are we in the Club?
Because we love to go to meals
Talk with our friends – it always feels
So good to talk and have fun times.

Why are we in the Club?
We love debate and discuss plans
Decide on projects – wear our bands
And know we make a difference.

Why are we in the Club?
So many reasons – the list goes on
The main one is because someone
Invited us!

Linda Beddows (SI The Fylde, England)

Mary Dalman *has lived in West Wickham, Kent, England for over 20 years. The focus of her career has been customer service in the private and local government sectors. She is an accredited assessor for the Institute of Customer Service. Mary is a member of SI Beckenham and District. She was Club President in 1995/6.*

*Mary co-lead the initial years of the Regional project on Personal
Safety on the Railways which was taken up at national level.
She is a member of Open Heart, Open Door with a particular
interest in international goodwill and understanding that has
taken her to North America and India on grants of friendship.*

Why a Soroptimist I am!

I'm a Soroptimist through and through
promoting our aims and ethos in yellow and blue.
All too often our light amongst ourselves we hide
when we should tell the world what we do with pride.

I value Soroptimist friendship, club must be 'give and take',
each of us contributes to the global difference S.I. makes.
We might think 'our little efforts' do not get us far
but all the programme focus forms show how dynamic we are.

International goodwill and understanding, the chance to learn
    and share
lobbying at all levels to make people more aware,
taking action on issues that are close to all our hearts,
working with like-minded committed people sets Soroptimists
    apart.

There's something in Soroptimism for everyone it seems
local service, international, programme focus themes.
We pool our strengths, play our roles and make a difference
    where we can
but learning, fun and friendship are also why a Soroptimist I
    am.

Mary Dalman (SI Beckenham and District, England)

Peta Edwards *was born in Sale Cheshire, England. After teaching for a number of years she changed direction to become a Manager of Fundraisers and then a freelance Funding and Marketing Consultant. Peta worked for several National, Regional and local charities which enabled her to work alongside some wonderful people. The building of relationships has always been her focus and was an essential element of her work. She was President of SI Garstang in 1999-2000. In the year of her Presidency, Peta got married,put plans in place to launch her new business and visited Australia! Peta's time as an active Soroptimist came to an end in 2007 when she moved to France. However, she looks back with fond memories of the friends she made and still has, within the movement. Throughout her life Peta has tried to encourage others to share her enthusiasm for projects. At the moment she has been asked to spearhead the recruitment of volunteers for a Cancer Charity in the Ariege, where she now lives, supporting English speaking cancer patients and their families. Peta strongly believes that it has always been a joy to see the difference we can make to the lives of others.*

Soroptimist Dream
To be read in the style of 'Albert and the Lion'

There's a famous location called Garstang
That's noted for friendship and fun.
And the folk in Soroptimists o'village
Get involved to ensure projects are done.

At first they were small but determined
To make their club a success.
Along with hard work and commitment
The numbers did swell…and regress.

Over't years they've grown not just in number
But in friendship, commitment and drive.

And to add to their list of attractions
They're also keen to survive.

Potential new members are trawled for
And invited for tea and a bun.
It's soon clear to them all that these members
Take part for friendship, support and good fun.

So onward the club it does travel
Winging its spirited way.
Sharing in projects and planning
With experience…and a bit of dismay.

Their success as a club is ongoing
With all the pride their tasks might entail.
So with a flourish of deep self-assurance
Into the future, with confidence they sail.
'Continue to invest in Programme Action'
Is the Soroptimist strategy and scheme.
The result is a community legacy
That is a reality and not just a dream.

Peta Edwards (France, formerly SI Carnforth, England)

Margaret Bush *was born in Surrey but spent most of her formative years in Leicester, England. She informs us that she is (just) the right side of 50 and has been happily married for 4 years to a wonderful man who loves her and her 2 tabby cats!She now works as a Senior Nurse Practitioner in a busy 'Walk–in' Centre in Folkestone, Kent. Margaret was invited to become a Soroptimist while working in Bridlington, East Yorkshire, where she made lifelong friends. Soroptimists also made life worthwhile when she moved to Kent in 2000 and did not know anyone. She says that she 'tortured' her club for 2 years as their President,while undertaking a BSc(Hons) degree. In 2010, Margaret will become the Regional President for the South East Region. She loves knitting and reading as well as travel. She is counting the weeks until she flies out to New Zealand to see her new godson!*

Soroptimists of Folkestone

I wear a little badge,
It's small and round and gold,
I've been a Soroptimist
Since I was 35 years old.

I love being in Soroptimism
It means so much to me,
There always is such optimism
It's lovely to be…involved!

The friendships means so much to me,
My husband's pleased to see,
Folkestone's such a lovely bunch,
With laughter and much glee.

Programme Action is the core,
Project Sierra's the quadrennial,
We don't know the women it's for

But the care will be perennial.

We help the victims of violence
Wherever that we can,
We hope to break the silence
When injured by a man.

We've a garden of remembrance
for parents who've lost a child.
It's at the Hawkinge cemetary,
We garden when it's mild!

All along Remembrance Road
We laid a hedge of rosemary.
It's loved by wildlife and toads
And locals who have memory(s).

I have a little badge,
It's round and small and gold,
I want to be a Soroptimist
'Till I'm 100 years old!

Margaret Bush (SI Folkestone, England)

Heather Swindlehurst *was born in Hillington, Norfolk, England. Even though she has lived most of her life in Lancashire, she still has a great affection for Norfolk. When asked what she would do if she ever won the lottery, she always says 'Buy a beach hut at Old Hunstanton', where she spent many happy family holidays. Heather now lives in Higham, a small Pendleside village. She has been married to Harry for 42 years, and they have two children and four grandchildren. Heather has always worked in finance; first for the Post Office, then the Midland Bank and since 1973 has run her own bookkeeping business. Heather is very involved with St Johns Church in Higham. She is a member of the choir, was Church Warden for 12 years, and is now the Verger. She is also Treasurer of the Easter Arts & Crafts Exhibition, which is now in its 38th year. Heather joined what was Colne & Nelson (now Pendleside) Soroptimists 24 years ago. She has served as Treasurer, and has also been Social Secretary. When Heather has time, she enjoys gardening.*

Soroptimists

Soroptimists, the best of sisters, see service supplied
Over all the world, no country denied.
Responsible women who get the job done.
Open minded, optimistic, who also have fun.
Projects completed with great endeavour,
Talents so varied, combining together...
Intent that our world be made safer for all,
Mindful of needs we hear every call.
Inspired by our sisters who went before
Seeking new members to be at our core.
Thankful for friendship, we firmly believe
Success guaranteed when teamwork achieved.

Heather Swindlehurst (SI Pendleside, England)

Anna Priest *was born in Dortmund, Germany, in 1935. She married Maurice Priest in 1956. After raising their four children she became a mature student at Manchester University. She taught Mathematics and Computer Studies (IT) in two Comprehensive Schools in Rochdale and Bradford. Anna became a member of SI Bacup. The club became SI Bacup and Rawtenstall in 1996 after amalgamation and SI Rossendale in 2004 after the closure of SI Haslingden. She was a member until very recently. Anna's hobbies include travel, going to the theatre, attending concerts of classical music, reading, patchwork and quilting.*

Soroptimists Care

Soroptimists care.
Soroptimists share.
Soroptimists dare
To make a difference.

Anna Priest (formerly SI Rossendale, England)

Val Christofferson *was born in London, England in 1926. At the age of ten, her family moved to Cape Town, South Africa, where she now lives. During World War 2 she served in the South African Women's Auxiliary Naval Service (SWANS). Val sang professionally for 27 years in the Chorus of Cape Town's Opera Company CAPAB (Cape Performing Arts Board). She is a member of U3A 'Pleasure and Education' and is currently presenting operas on DVD to interested members. Val has also specialized in Financial Planning, Estate Planning, Wills and Tax Planning and has spoken widely to groups of women on 'Women and Finance'. She was Manager of a branch of 'Syfrets' in Cape Town, a long-established historical Trust Company. She is a founder of the Belmont Care Centre for Mentally Challenged young people and has run a Recreation Club for teenagers in this category. She has raised funds to buy a Residential Care Centre which now houses 7 adults. Val married a Dane and lived in Denmark for a while, forming a special affinity for the country and its people. She reads, writes and speaks Danish. She is now a widow. with 2 children and 3 grandchildren who live in Australia. Val has been* **a** *Member of SI Cape of Good Hope for 23 years where she has served as Club President, Treasurer and Secretary. She is currently Friendship Link Co-ordinator and serves on a sub-committee for the anti-trafficking of women and children. Val served for two years as National Secretary for Soroptimist International of South Africa (SISA). She received a 'Soroptimist of the Year' Award in 2006. Her hobbies include playing indifferent Bridge and Mahjong!*

Nkosi Sikilel' iAfrika

Proud and tall and gracious stands majestic Table Mountain
Below the city nestles and greets with spraying fountain
Two oceans beat upon her shores – the Indian and Atlantic
And balmy, palm-decked promenades enchant the more
   romantic.

'Bon Esperance' our Cape was named by navigators past
'Good Hope' this Cape is called today – a name that will hold
   fast
Diverse in population of many cultures made
So colourful and musical it **is** a grand parade.

  The problems of Society creep through our city streets
  Hands held in supplication at every corner greets.

A band of steadfast women bring HOPE into their midst
Worldwide their sisters labour, are called 'Soroptimists'
The rights of every woman, child, the first consideration
Their Health, their Education, throughout this widespread
   nation.

And at this tip of Africa we turn our faces North
To where another challenge waits – where fruits of war brought
   forth
Fragmented lives in Freetown, Kamakwe and Mattru
A Project called SIERRA – a call to me and you

To find it there within us to go that extra mile
Bringing HOPE and HOMES to families, turn tears into a
   smile
And pray that they will always receive their daily bread
Remembering, in the meanwhile, by Whom that prayer was
   said.

Val Christofferson (SI Cape of Good Hope, South Africa)

Index by poet

POETS

as featured on the rear cover *(from left to right)*

Top row : Jacque Emery, Audrey Harper, Imre Irten, Bernadette
    Archuletta, Ashlee Austin, Lois Herman, Mary Ndlovu,
    Guzin Senbas, Hilary Semple.

Second row: Pansy Griffith, Irene Morris, Olwen Jones, Pat
    Fergusson, Poco Davis, Anne Quainoo, Gisela Hertel,
    Sharon Lenahan, Chris Knight.

Third row: Wendy Grimshaw, Jacqueline Pilot, Mary Clark,
    Penny Luker, Su Rennison, Ruth Puddick, Linda Beddows,
    Jeri Bawden, Annamarie Megrdichian.

Fourth row: Hannah Lurie, Joan Lees, Brenda Escreet, Deborah
    Stojevich, Erene Grieve, Sandra Donald, Tracey Lowther,
    Gloria Hill, Linda Glaser.

Fifth row: Peta Edwards, Kris Pearson, Kathy McElvany, Carol
    Salter, Sue Berry, Sally Shears, Marie Blacktop, Hilary
    Allinson, Sheila Eustace.

Sixth row: Ann Reeves, Jill Lazard, Carolyn Lowe, Moya
    Coates, Bronwyn O'Shannessy, June Gabbitas, Peggy van
    Meter, Anna Priest, Val Christofferson.

Bottom row : Betty Martin, Anne Pickup, Heather
    Swindlehurst, Florence Evans, Mary Dalman, Frances
    Meech, Clare Harding.